HOW TO FIND THE TRUE SELF WITHIN

SECRETS OF RELIEVING STRESS AND ANXIETY

HOW TO FIND THE TRUE SELF WITHIN

SECRETS OF RELIEVING STRESS AND ANXIETY

Mary Sidhwani, RN/PsyD, CCH

Printed in the United States of America
First Printing, 2019

ISBN: 9781076421449

CONTENTS

"Do you know what you are? You are a manuscript of a divine letter, you are a mirror reflecting a noble face. This Universe is not outside of you. Look inside yourself. Everything that you want, you are already that." ---Rumi

INTRODUCTION

"All that we are is a result of what we have thought.
The mind is everything.
What we think, we become."
----- Buddha (563-483 B.C.)

Who am I really? Why can't I reach my goals in life? Why am I so stressed and anxious? What is it that would make me truly happy? These questions, among others, are those we ask ourselves at some point in our lives. Sometimes these questions arise spontaneously, other times they are triggered by a significant or traumatic life event. We begin to wonder who we really are beneath the layers of old resentments, stories, expectations of others, hurts, injustices, trauma and so forth. These questions beg us to answer what would make us truly happy, content, fulfilled. What is our true path, purpose and passion, what is the truth within us?

I have asked these questions of myself in the past and as a hypnotherapist of many years, I have had the privilege of assisting others on their own journeys of discovery and inner peace. Through my experience as a hypnotherapist, I believe it is essential to discover ways to reduce stress and promote relaxation. During the ups and downs which are a part of everyday life, we begin to feel stressed and overwhelmed. Some days we struggle more than others to find our balance, wondering how we can cope with the demands and challenges we encounter throughout the day.

When we are stressed and overwhelmed, everything spins out of control. Literally hundreds of factors can cause stress; from noise to resentment, from lack of sleep to poor diet, from fatigue to emotional turmoil. Through my education and experience, I have come to understand the great importance of shifting out of the stress response as soon as possible. When the stress response is triggered, the nervous system responds by releasing a flood of stress hormones including adrenaline, cortisol and norepinephrine by activating what is known as the HPA axis. This axis involves a complex set of relationships and signals that exist between the hypothalamus, pituitary and adrenals. Prolonged stress overwhelms the adrenal glands and causes other negative effects such a reduced immunity, headaches, digestive issues, and insomnia among others which interfere with the healthy programming of the body.

Opportunities abound to find ways to reduce stress and anxiety and find that true self within. An anxious person could explore yoga, meditation, exercise, mindfulness, attend workshops and/or read books that demonstrate how best to reduce stress and anxiety.

Not only must we learn how to reduce stress and anxiety in our lives but also to discover who we truly are and what brings joy and purpose into our lives. Basically, what lights us up. With that in mind, I felt guided to write this book which incorporates the principles of hypnosis, among other techniques in order to help others discover their true self within. This discovery allows us to bring forth an abiding sense of inner peace, balance and calmness in our daily lives.

Through my experiences personally and professionally, I believe discovery and belief in our true selves is the first stage of our healing. As we explore these opportunities together, we will learn more about our true selves throughout the book. True self is also known as the higher self. Healing begins as we recognize the truth of a higher self residing within us. We all have a true self, it knows our true path, purpose and passion. As we connect to this true self it assists us in recognizing what needs to be healed. It sheds a light on the parts of self that are perhaps operating in less functional ways.

The series of healing from anxiety and stress begins with realizing we have a true self. We may already understand this intellectually, however, as we process through these steps in healing, we will come to know it and align with it experientially. As we apply the processes described in each chapter, we will experience this for ourselves. Everyone is unique and each individual comes to a deeper knowing and understanding of this true self at different stages. However, everyone comes to this knowing as they journey inward during this time of self-discovery and change. As we begin to acquaint and later align with our own true selves, we will discover the gift of peace.

I would like to share a bit in this introduction about how I found this truth within myself. As I healed from anxiety and stress, I felt compelled to write this book and help others on their journey to discovering their true self.

For more than eighteen years, I have had the honor as a therapist to assist clients on their healing journey. For approximately thirteen years prior to becoming a therapist, I served as a Registered Nurse. I held two long-term positions, the first at a residential treatment center for children who experienced abuse and neglect. The second was at a facility which owned multiple group homes for developmentally disabled adults. Though I loved being a nurse, each of these positions carried great responsibility, long hours and required being on call throughout the night without compensation. I found myself becoming mentally, emotionally and physically exhausted. My stress and anxiety levels continued to increase.

Even when not working, I couldn't seem to quiet my mind and I did not know where to turn or how to heal. This led me to think about which aspects of nursing I still loved and found fulfilling. As I considered my options, I realized I most enjoyed my one on one time with my patients. The most rewarding moments occurred when I could spend time listening, counseling and guiding them. As I researched viable options, I felt drawn to a graduate program in counseling and women's health. Upon beginning classes in the graduate program, I noticed electives in hypnotherapy. I became instantly hooked and felt as if I had come home.

I do not know how to otherwise describe my thoughts and feelings. I experienced the hypnotic state many times during class sessions and began to make profound healing shifts within. As I experienced hypnosis, I began to recognize the truth within myself. My life began to subtly shift in a very positive way. I began to feel calm, and to heal from the intense stress of my nursing position.

Since my immune system had been affected by the long hours, constant interrupted sleep from being on call throughout the night and the intense stress of my position and responsibilities, for years I experienced continual colds, stomach viruses, fatigue, and migraine headaches. The mind/body connection is powerful, so the healing hypnosis sessions brought about an improvement in my health.

My confidence and calmness increased more and more as each day passed. One day, as I prepared a speech which I had volunteered to do for class, something I never would have agreed to prior to hypnosis, feelings of gratitude and blessings overwhelmed me. I realized how my life had transformed dramatically yet it had unfolded in a series of gentle steps. Each one leading me higher and higher to new levels of consciousness and understanding. I saw that the wisdom of the truth within was buried beneath layers of hurt, anger, resentment, and old stories. False stories about who I was and my capabilities along with the opinions of others about who I should be and what I could accomplish.

Through hypnosis, I removed blocks, and unleashed shackles, beginning to build upon beautiful resources, strengths, gifts and capabilities that had resided within all along. I began more and more to identify with this authentic, true self as I tapped into the consciousness of my own true beauty and worth. At that point I knew I would be extremely honored and privileged to help others transform their lives and recognize the truth, the beauty, the worth, the gifts, the passion and purpose which lies within each of us. A great desire, purpose and passion to do this for others overtook me. Though I had tried other healing modalities, the experience of hypnosis; learning the power of the mind and other healing techniques which I describe in this book, ultimately brought the most profound and lasting results.

Unfortunately, many people today are not living a life of peace, joy, and alignment with higher self but are experiencing the symptoms of stress, pain, woundedness and anxiety. The energy of this stress transverses our bodies and interferes with the healthy functioning of the mind/body/spirit. Through my experience, I have observed that no matter the client's issue, their healing followed a certain pattern. I also realized that my own healing had also followed this same pattern. Healing which leads to a life free of anxiety and stress, allowing us to easily cope with whatever arises so that we may come from this place of inner peace. I became aware of this how this process unfolded into a series of inner healing.

Several years ago, I developed the guided hypnosis audio series: "Recognize the Truth Within," based on this process of inner healing. Due to the kind response and feedback from others on how this series benefited them, I felt the need to create a more comprehensive written version, describing this healing pattern in depth. Each chapter reflects, describes and examines this healing process.

In chapter one, "Recognize the Truth Within," we begin to understand the importance of coming home to self. We begin to align with the truth of who we really are. What lies beneath the layers of hurt, negative thoughts, beliefs, and experiences. I received a wonderful message from someone who shared her experience after listening to the "Recognize the Truth Within" recording. She relayed that as she drifted into the hypnotic state, she suddenly saw her true self. Her true self was radiant and provided guidance as to how to pursue her goals and dreams. She expressed great joy in knowing that she connected to this powerful part of herself to collaborate with as she moves forward in life.

In "Creating a Healing Space," the second chapter, we begin to create a healing space we can return to again and again, creating this safe sanctuary for self as we continue to heal.

The third chapter, "Healing from Anger and Resentment," describes the healing which takes place as we begin to release the layers of anger and resentment. These layers prevent us from seeing the true beauty and worth that lies within. We forgive others and self for anything that happened with or without malintent along with any regrets about it. Forgiveness does not mean we condone traumatic events but that we cease to allow ourselves to be a victim, a puppet to the old recordings and triggers. No longer allowing others the power to continue to impact our lives in a negative or unhealthy way.

As we remove the old layers of anger and move toward forgiveness, we move more deeply into our heart and discover the child within. In the fourth chapter, "Nurturing Your Inner Child," we discover the child's gifts of joy, creativity, spontaneity and lightness of being.

Accepting and loving that child leads to the next process of loving and honoring self, which is described in the following chapter, "Loving and Accepting Self." This is a beautiful and incredible healing to witness.

Loving and accepting self leads us to the sixth process of healing, "Living With Inner Peace." As we honor, love and accept self, we can live with and come from this place of inner peace. We recognize the truth that peace lies within our very core, abiding thought the ups and downs of everyday life as we recognize this great truth which lies within each of us.

This book will teach us to use hypnotic principles to access all three levels of the mind in order to heal. We heal on the conscious, unconscious and spirit consciousness levels. We will learn about these three levels of the mind and how we do heal on each of these levels. Spiritual writing tells us, " You can be transformed by the renewing of your mind."

Believing in the inherent truth of that statement, my intention is to help others understand that as we renew our minds with thoughts and ideas based on self-love, self-worth, self-esteem and self-respect, we begin to create a new blueprint for our life. Using the power of the unconscious mind to transform victimhood and shed the bindings of the old outdated recordings, especially those that keep us stuck in old ways of being and doing. By focusing our intentions on creating new neural pathways, we become free of anxiety and stress, bringing forth peacefulness and calmness in all aspects of our daily lives and connecting us to our true self.

Finally, I would like to share tips on using the various techniques and tools described in each chapter, so you may easily refer to this chapter as needed.

Reader Tips for Affirmations:

1. Affirmations are used in your daily self-hypnosis practice but can also be used on their own throughout the day.

2. Choose two or three affirmations from a chapter and read each affirmation three times either silently or aloud.

3. It is most helpful to use the affirmations in order as given in the chapters, however, please utilize the affirmations in whichever order feels right to you.

4. Stay with the same two or three affirmations for at least eight to twelve weeks.

5. In addition to your daily self-hypnosis practice, it is beneficial to read each affirmation three times in a row, several times a day. Make sure to do so before bed since it is a very powerful time. Reading the affirmations five minutes before sleep, allows the subconscious to imprint these powerful, healing suggestions into the mind.

6. If you choose to read the affirmations aloud, it is helpful to do so in a confident voice.

7. To add more power to the positive affirmations, write it down as you speak it.

8. It is also helpful to post your affirmations in areas where you will see them often. For example, put your affirmations on a sticky note on your desk, drawer, mirror, nightstand, refrigerator, car dashboard, or computer monitor. You can also slip it

into your wallet or carry a small notebook with you.

9. It is also helpful to look at yourself directly in the mirror and say each affirmation out loud during this time. The unconscious mind learns through repetition, thus repeating your affirmations while doing this 'mirror work' is very powerful.

10. Your affirmations will slowly help the mind to confront the disconnect between what you are saying and how you see yourself. Repeating the affirmations helps retrain the mind to feel comfortable and at ease when you think in a positive way.

Reader Guide to Self -Hypnosis:

1. Read over each affirmation three times.

2. Sit down or lie down in a comfortable position and close your eyes.

3. Take a nice slow breath in and let it out slowly five times.

4. Raise your index finger on either hand, then bring it down slowly.

5. Count backwards from five to one.

6. Put your thumb and index finger together, on either hand and allow yourself to relax.

7. Think to yourself this phrase: "I am completely relaxed."

8. As you drift deeper, see yourself achieving your goal. See yourself with your new patterns of behavior. Hear yourself saying to others how the

new, positive behavior is working in your life. Allow yourself to feel the difference as you achieve the goal you set for yourself.

9. When you are ready, simply count from one to five or set a time to alert you. Tell yourself when you open your eyes, you will be back in a fully aware, alert rested and refreshed.

Reader Tips for Practicing Self-Hypnosis

1. Please practice your self-hypnosis daily. Just fifteen minutes of hypnosis is equivalent to one hour of deep restful sleep. It is also a centering and grounding process as well as increased the production of the neurotransmitter serotonin. This is known as the 'feel good' chemical which promotes feelings of safety, security and happiness. It also promotes sound restful sleep, decreases stress and increases memory and concentration.

2. You can practice your self-hypnosis in the morning. Some people prefer this and set their alarm fifteen minutes earlier than usual in order to work in their practice. Alternatively, you may prefer to practice self-hypnosis prior to bedtime or at any time that is best for you. It is easier to incorporate the habit of self-hypnosis if it is practiced approximately the same time and place each day.

3. The key to success with your practice is to do self-hypnosis daily.

4. It takes repetition of healthy, positive affirmations given in self-hypnosis before the old programming

11

lets go. Please be patient with yourself during this process.

5. The old negative programming will let go as you practice self-hypnosis. It is very important to give yourself credit for even the most subtle of changes. This indicates the changes are taking root and are beginning to grow and flourish in your life.

Reader Tips for Visualizations

1. You may wish to record the visualization on the voice memo feature on your phone or another device.

2. Find a quiet, comfortable place to sit or lie down, close your eyes and begin breathing in deeply and exhaling slowly five times.

3. You may wish to set a timer for as long as you wish to do the visualization, at least fifteen minutes is preferable.

4. The unconscious mind cannot tell the difference between a visualization and an actual event. They work better when you believe they will work. However, a visualization will work whether you totally believe or not. Visualizations will work faster and better when you believe in them.

5. When using any of the visualizations, bring in as many of the five senses as you can. Make it very detailed. Create the scene in your mind as you see yourself with the new healthy patterns. Hear yourself saying to others how the new positive patterns are working in your life. Allow yourself to feel the difference.

6. Use the visualization in each chapter at least once a week. The more often you use the visualization, the more quickly the mind will learn this new way of knowing and being.

7. Visualization is a powerful proven technique for refining your self-image and making important changes in your life. When you visualize positive, healthy changes, you begin to manifest it into your life.

Reader Tips for Using the Meditations

1. It may be helpful to read the meditations aloud as you record them on the voice memo feature on your phone or other device. If you choose to do this, please read the words slowly and calmly.

2. Playing soothing music in the background helps the mind to relax.

3. Find a quiet, comfortable place to sit or lie down. Close your eyes and breathe in deeply and exhale slowly five times prior to doing the meditation.

4. Doing the meditation at least once a week is very beneficial.

5. Stay with whatever arises. When thoughts or feelings arise, stay with them and allow the words of the guided meditation to carry you through.

6. Don't worry about clearing the mind. If thoughts come to you during the meditation, just let them come and then let them go as if they are birds or clouds passing through.

7. Develop a loving attitude. When you note

thoughts and feelings arising during a meditation, look at them with a loving, friendly attitude. They are a part of you and are coming up in order to be acknowledged and healed. Allow the process without judgment.

Further guided meditation recordings may be found on my website: **www.womenstherapeutic.com**

If you wish to find a qualified hypnotherapist, please visit the American Society of Clinical Hypnosis website: **www.asch.net**

CHAPTER ONE

"Recognize the Truth Within"

"I am at peace with myself and with the universe."
**"I am now easily allowing outside stress to dissolve
and fade away."**
**"I am more relaxed each day and this allows me to
heal and to connect to my true self."**

During the hypnotic state, whether in private session, self-hypnosis, or listening to a recording, we can speak directly to the unconscious mind. Past negative experiences are difficult to challenge with the logic of the conscious mind, however, in hypnosis we are directly communicating with the unconscious mind and beginning to challenge those long-held negative beliefs. We can begin to explore, examine and review that which has been held in the unconscious mind. As we do this, the unconscious mind begins to release, reframe and remove blocks and fears. It removes the illusions so we can see clearly in order to live a life of peace, joy, and fulfillment. We begin to connect to the true self which lies within.

In Proverbs it says: "As a man thinketh in his heart so is he." The word 'heart' in this context refers not to the physical heart, but instead is used symbolically to refer to the seat of the emotions, the inner mind, the unconscious mind.

Long before Freud was born, these words from Proverbs explained that what determines our outlook on life, our health and wellbeing, was not what we say or think consciously but what we think or say in our 'heart' or unconsciously. So how can the unconscious mind be reached and re-educated? Once again, I believe the most effective way is through the proper use of hypnosis and self-hypnosis along with the various techniques and tools I will describe in the coming chapters.

The unconscious mind learns through repetition and so as we continue to experience the hypnotic state and apply the tools and techniques presented here, we then program the unconscious mind with positive, life affirming and changing thoughts. Thus, bringing into our lives what we so desire and bringing this healing into every aspect of our lives in very powerful and positive ways. Discovering that I wanted to help others experience this profound healing, led me to change my concentration to a master's in clinical hypnotherapy. Several years later, I completed my doctorate in counseling psychology in order to delve even more deeply into the workings of the inner mind and understand it.

In the graduate program, my mentor, Dr. Winkler, was insightful and creative bringing great wisdom through his years of experience. I was enthralled and captivated as I learned of the various levels of the mind and the transformation brought about through the utilization of hypnosis. I learned we healed on all three levels of the mind: consciously, unconsciously and on the level of spirit consciousness.

The conscious mind is the thinking mind, and it is involved with our constant thoughts, everyday actions, logic and judgment. It is analytical, reasoning and intellectual. I recall being stunned when I learned this level of the mind holds only 10% of our power. 90% of our power comes from the unconscious mind. The unconscious mind is like a huge DVD, a database, a search engine or storage house of all life experiences, traumas, fears, events, emotional obstacles, imprints, impressions, beliefs and is also the level of the mind which receives suggestions. The conscious and unconscious levels of the mind are also likened to an iceberg; the tip of the iceberg, that which is visible is the conscious mind and the enormous mass of the iceberg which lies invisible beneath the surface of the water is the unconscious mind.

As a nurse, I understood the great power of the unconscious mind as it controls a multitude of processes in the body. This level of the mind never sleeps, it keeps our heart beating, hair growing, food digesting, cells repairing and many, many other processes without any conscious awareness or effort on our part.

The unconscious mind has received and recorded everything that has ever happened to us since we came into existence. Though we do not consciously recall all of these things, the unconscious mind remembers, and we are actually behaving from these imprints, impressions, thoughts, ideas, beliefs and experiences. It is as if a computer program is continuously running yet we are not consciously aware of all that exists within that programming. When we go within during hypnosis, we are accessing the unconscious mind and communicating with this level in order to remove blocks and to utilize the power of unconscious to cease being a victim to old outdated recordings, especially those which have kept us stuck within old paradigms. Once we tap into that supreme power, we are free to love, nurture, nourish and find the truth within ourselves.

Spirit consciousness is the third level of the mind and is also where the higher self resides. The bridge from conscious mind to spirit consciousness is the unconscious mind. This level of the mind encompasses the energy of light, love, wisdom, peace, compassion, forgiveness, bliss and enlightenment. It is also known as the 'crown jewel' state because the higher self resides there with all the great expansive state of consciousness that creates true spiritual healing power, leading to knowing the true self and living a life of peace.

We heal on all three levels of the mind: conscious mind, unconscious mind and on the level of spirit consciousness. As discussed previously, the conscious mind is the thinking mind, it is intellectual, analytical, logical, judging and reasoning. This part of the mind can often be very negative. For example, when a client sees me for the first time, the conscious mind is the part of self that may say: "Why am I here?" "Nothing has worked for me, so this probably will not work too." "Am I wasting my time?"

Since I am aware of this, I mention during the initial meeting that negative thoughts may be going through the conscious mind and that is okay. Clients are safe and free to ask me any questions and to relay any intrusive thoughts that may be coming up for them. I spend as much time as needed to answer questions, allay fears, clear up misconceptions and dispel myths surrounding hypnosis. This helps the conscious mind to be more at ease; more open and receptive to the process.

I also see the conscious mind coming forth during initial sessions. For example, while guiding a client to a memory connected to the issue in need of healing, she suddenly became aware of a childhood memory and subsequent memories. Later, she asked me if she just made it all up, or 'forced' herself to come up with something. Again, it is the conscious mind bringing in negativity and doubts. I reassured the client that her unconscious mind brought forth exactly what needed to come forth. Also, I explained that at times the thoughts that come forth during session may not make sense to conscious mind, however, very often those are the thoughts/memories that have the most significant impact on healing.

The language of the unconscious mind is very often in the form of symbols. For example, the unconscious mind is involved in our dreaming state. How else would it communicate to us then through our imagination? As the client progresses in healing, they experience the healing shifts in their life, they more and more trust what the unconscious mind brings forth during sessions. Also, it is beautiful to see how this parallels with clients trusting themselves, moving into self-trust and self-belief more and more in their daily lives.

I would like to expand more on this role of imagination in the hypnotic process. Many times when I think of imagination, I recall the words of the Roman philosopher Seneca saying, "We suffer more from imagination than from reality." We have the blessing and perhaps we can say the difficulty of having an imagination. For example, we can excessively worry which quickly leads to endless rumination of all that can go wrong. The vividness of our imagination can terrify us and the body responds to this fear by releasing the stress hormones adrenaline and cortisol. So we can use our imagination to hold ourselves hostage or to set ourselves free. We can focus on fear or we can focus on joy and gratitude.

Either way, focusing on fear or focusing on joy, we're imagining. We have the power to choose what we imagine. We can also choose to limit the ability of our imagination or we can choose to allow our imagination to be limitless. Using our imagination can be a wonderfully creative process and very powerful while in the trance state.

Studies at Stanford University have proven via PET scans that the brain reacts the same way whether something is real or imagined. For example, the brain will light up exactly the same way if it sees the color red or imagines the color red. Thus, the use of imagination in hypnosis is extremely powerful. Using our imagination can be a wonderfully creative process and very powerful while in the trance state.

For example, a client, Kim, was very anxious about an upcoming job interview. She had been using the power of her imagination to envision the meeting not going well. Each time she thought of the interview, she felt nauseated, shaky and very anxious. Her imagination was really working! Kim imagined what this interview was going to be like, running it continuously over and over in her mind. She succeeded in creating thoughts and feelings of anxiety and negative imaginings of the interview process.

Actually, Kim did not believe she had a very good imagination. Many times clients will come to me saying this very thing, they believe they do not have a good imagination. I then ask them to please describe to me how they ride a bike, swing a golf club, knit a scarf, prepare a meal or brush their teeth. They quickly use their memory and imagination to tell me the steps involved. With our imagination we solve problems and all the technological advances and inventions we enjoy were just a thought in some person's mind before they came into reality. This ability to imagine has helped us to survive and thrive.

Everyone has the ability to imagine, it is part of who we truly are. So instead of waiting for something unusual or remarkable to happen, we can approach imagining as an opportunity to discern more closely how our imagination operates.

Kim was rather shocked when she understood that she had successfully imagined this negative scenario with all the resulting symptoms of anxiety. She realized she actually did have a very powerful and vivid imagination. I suggested that she was so good at imagining that we would use our session to turn her negative process around and get a real sense of just what her imagination was capable of doing for her in a positive and productive way.

We did session work around imagining herself calm and confident when thinking about the interview, using her powerful imagination to see and feel herself calm and in control during the interview process. We mentally rehearsed this several times while in hypnosis. Many suggestions were given to overcome feelings of anxiety and panic around the process and instead plan what she was going to say so she could feel really prepared.

Suggestions were also incorporated to research the position, helping Kim come up with factual information and good questions to ask. Post session, Kim utilized self-hypnosis to give herself suggestions to be calm, relaxed and in control whenever she thought of the interview and while at the interview. She imagined herself poised, calm and confident throughout the interview process. Kim later emailed me that the interview went extremely well. Approximately two weeks later I received another message saying she was offered the position. She was so happy and said she would never again doubt her ability to use her powerful imagination!

In hypnosis, imagery comes without conscious effort. As one enters hypnosis, they set an intention of what they wish to achieve in the hypnotic state. For example, to remember something, to solve something, release something, etc. Then, while in hypnosis, to observe passively what imagery occurs on its own, without exerting conscious effort. The unconscious responds more readily to imagination (guided imagery) than to hypnotic suggestions. When hypnotic suggestions are used, their greatest effect is not in their literal meanings, but in the imagined thoughts they produce. Words and phrases can produce powerful imagery, so a thoughtful hypnotherapist will be sensitive to the imagery that certain words may trigger in the imagination.

Part of the task of the hypnotherapist is to determine what words are cues for specific imagery for the client.

This comes about as a result of the conversations with the client, i.e., their preferences, experiences, opinions, beliefs and so on. When using imagery in hypnosis, the client's own recollections are more impactful than a newly created image. For example, to help someone increase confidence in public speaking, it is more effective to use their actual memories of times when they felt confident in speaking or otherwise, than to describe an idealized image to which they cannot relate from personal experience. Doing so will help the client to accept this imagery more readily using all the five senses. Imagination can be visual, auditory, olfactory (smell) gustatory (taste) and/or tactile (physical sensations). Paying attention to colors, shapes, faces, attire, landscape, sounds, feelings. It's important to be patient, not rush it, or make hard work of it. It's good to know our unconscious mind can take care of us. We can just relax, and the unconscious mind knows just how to do this, just how to bring up the right scene, thought, memory or event.

Why have our unconscious minds imagine symptoms of anxiety, fear, worry or panic, when with practice in the hypnotic trance state, we can imagine feeling comfortable and worry free. As we utilize hypnosis in session work, or during self-hypnosis, or while listening to a hypnotic recording or while engaged in a healing visualization or meditation, we can discover for ourselves just how powerful our imagination is and put it to powerful and positive work for our highest good.

I would like to share one more example of how the conscious level of the mind may come forth during the hypnotic process. This also ties into our knowledge about imagination and the fear it can produce. Years ago, a new client was very excited about her first session. Donna had heard me present several times at NASA Goddard Space Center in Greenbelt, MD. She kindly contacted me to help her overcome a long-standing issue in her life.

As with all new clients, we spent quite a bit of time discussing hypnosis and answering any questions she had. Donna assured me that we had covered everything she had wanted to ask and felt very excited about the session. As she drifted down deeply into hypnosis, I was just above to move forward within the session when she suddenly opened her eyes and exclaimed, "I lost you!" I reassured her and reminded her that when one drifts into hypnosis they may go into a light trance state and hear everything said, or go into a medium trance and drift down and then up into a lighter state or they may drift into a very deep state and completely lose the sound of my voice 'consciously' yet the unconscious mind will always hear, receive and remember what took place. I felt there was a fear of losing control and so we discussed/reviewed this in depth.

She assured me she felt very safe and wanted to continue the session. Yet, Donna continually brought herself out of hypnosis each time she drifted down deeply. I could feel and sense the conscious mind wanting to be in control and not allowing the unconscious mind to come forth more strongly. We discussed everything in depth and her next visit was very enlightening. When Donna returned, she relayed she had traveled to Las Vegas. While there, she, her spouse and daughter attended a lay hypnotist show. Her daughter recorded her parents going onto the stage to join the other participants. Everyone was going along with the act except for Donna. She said that the hypnotist tapped her on the shoulder and asked her to leave the stage as she was 'ruining the act!' She realized it was her fear of losing control and saw how the conscious mind was negating what we had discussed. Donna imagined 'losing me' and being controlled in some way if her conscious mind was not active and alert.

Now that she had that experience in Las Vegas, her conscious mind allowed her to go into a trance state knowing she could never be forced to do anything against her will, or become controlled in any way. Donna easily entered the trance state and progressed very well.

The unconscious mind, as stated previously, is a very powerful part of our mind. It is the repository for all life experiences (including past lifetimes), traumas, fears, events, emotional obstacles, imprints, impressions, beliefs and the receiver of suggestions. Once again, though we do not consciously recall all these things, the unconscious mind remembers and operates and forms belief systems based on all this information. During hypnosis, we are accessing this level of the mind and communicating, examining, exploring, assessing, reframing and releasing all that no longer serves us. However, we still retain all lessons/learning for no matter how unpleasant, often that uncomfortable emotion teaches us valuable lessons.

I have had the privilege of helping many beloved souls on their healing journey. Through all of the many sessions and years, whenever I think of how to exemplify the power of the unconscious mind and the power of hypnosis one special client comes to mind. Initially, the client's husband contacted me asking if I would help his wife with a 'bird phobia'. I relayed that I would be honored to help her with the issue. A lovely person arrived, and she spoke all about her intense fear of birds. Melissa was four years of age when this phobia began and was sixty-seven at the time she came to me. It brought to mind how very powerful the unconscious mind is, since it held on to this intense fear for sixty-three years. In fact, the fear only escalated as the years progressed.

As I did the initial intake, Melissa relayed that she and her husband were extremely concerned. Whenever she saw a bid, terror gripped Melissa in its iron fist, driving her to put herself in harm's way. She even took to running into traffic or into a parking lot if she saw a bird. Her family had a condo at the beach, and she would leave her husband, children and grandchildren and return to the condo whenever a seagull would land near her. This phobia was greatly impacting the quality of Melissa's life.

We first worked on her anxiety and stress surrounding the phobia. She did very well and was so pleased that her co-workers, family and friends commented on the peace and calm she exuded. At approximately the fifth session, I felt we were ready to really delve into the regression work. That is, going back to when this phobia was first created. Then to have the unconscious mind explore, examine and assess all that created the phobia. Thus, we did a regression technique back to the time just before the phobia began. Melissa saw herself as a four year old little girl. It was fascinating because she could only see from the eye level of a four year old. She saw two women standing next to her, whom she knew they were her mother and aunt. She saw many, many feathers in the street, along with the sounds of birds squawking and people screaming. Her mother placed her arm in front of her and pushed her back onto the sidewalk.

I took my time talking to the unconscious mind and thanking it for protecting her all these years. However, that time has passed, and Melissa is now safe. The overprotection of the unconscious mind, which caused the phobia, was actually placing her in harm's way now since Melissa would run out into traffic, etc. in order to escape from a bird. Also, it was causing great distress to her because she could not fully enjoy her life.

Tapping into the power of her unconscious mind, I asked if it could release her from the phobia knowing that she is safe now. The unconscious mind relayed that 'yes' it had completely released her from the cause of that problem. I thanked it very much for its past protection, for its communication and for releasing the client from the intense fear which had plagued her.

Afterwards, Melissa said she felt as if a huge weight had been lifted from her. It brought me such joy to see her radiant and filled with peace and happiness. Approximately one month later she left me an excited voice mail. She said that her husband had taken her to a dinner show. During the show a hawk was released into the audience. Her husband instinctively took her hand and said not to worry, they would leave right away. Melissa told her husband she was fine, that she didn't like the bird but was no longer afraid of it. I could hear the pride, the relief and joy in her voice. I was so grateful to have been a part of the healing.

As Melissa accessed her unconscious mind, she was released from this long-standing issue. She was able to find, and to recognize the truth within herself. Underneath all the layers of pain, anxiety, fear and stress, she was actually a very calm, peaceful and confident woman. Melissa reconnected to the truth which resided at the very core of her being. No longer identifying with her pain and woundedness, and allowing her true, radiant self to come forth strongly.

The unconscious mind is also the bridge between the conscious mind and Spirit consciousness. As we continue to remove the layers of pain, hurt, negative imprints, thoughts, beliefs, and experiences from the unconscious, we then create a clear connection to the level of spirit consciousness. This is where the Higher Self resides. I believe that the goal of each existence, is to forge a strong connection to higher self. At this level, the truth within each of us resides.

Many times clients have asked me to explain the difference between higher self and soul self. It can be a very complicated and esoteric subject and I have done my best to understand and impart that knowledge. Through years of education, reading and experience, I feel that the soul is the part of us that evolves in time and space. I also see soul as connected with the inner child. The inner child within us has been wounded through various experiences as we grow. As we learn how to heal the inner child, we are also healing the soul. For the soul can also then let go of the woundedness and retain all lessons and learning on its journey. Just as the inner child transforms within, the soul too evolves and grows in wisdom, truth and a greater understanding of its purpose and path. The soul is 'clothed' in garments of the four lower bodies. These four lower bodies are known as our four energy fields, or 'sheaths' of consciousness. They surround our soul and function as our vehicles of expression in the material world.

Aside from the physical body, we have an emotional body containing our feelings and desires. We also have a mental body, the body of thinking and reasoning. As well as the spiritual body, which is the highest vibrating of the four and contains all life memories. When these four bodies are aligned, the light of our higher self can flow freely through us. So in order to recognize the truth within, to align with our true higher self, we need to gain balance in all these bodies: mentally, physically, emotionally and spiritually. Through the principles and application of hypnotic techniques, we can heal on all these four levels. As we do so, the soul heals from hurtful and harmful experiences, so it can then connect to the higher self, recognizing the true self.

Higher self is when we, as the personality self, can express our light of the divine self through our words, thoughts and actions and all that we are and do. We need to give great loving care to our self, or unfortunately, we can create self-neglect, not knowing who we truly are, living a life of pain and woundedness. Or we can delve into the unconscious mind which holds all our life experiences and heal the wounds, the pain, the untruth of who we think we are and what we can accomplish. Through healing the pain which resides in the unconscious mind, we are loving, protecting, and guiding our ourselves to reunion with our higher self, our true self.

The higher self resides on the level of spirit consciousness. Again, I believe that the universal lesson for all souls is to find the spiritual self, the higher self, the true self. We can only find true peace, truth, joy and happiness by re-connecting with our higher self and listening to our higher self's guidance. Learning this truth, allows us to live our lives in joy. Our higher self is a perfect instrument through which our soul can express itself on the earthly plane. As our higher self, we can carry out our soul's purpose, recognizing and bringing forth our true purpose and self. Rather than following the desires of the personality self, we can then align with our true self, our true purpose and recognize the truth which lies within each of us.

Hypnosis, very simply put, is a very relaxed state of mind. The hypnotherapist does not 'put us into a trance' but guides the client into a very relaxed, calm, and peaceful state of mind. When I see a client for an initial session, I spend as much time as needed clearing up any misconceptions, myths or fears surrounding hypnosis. The most important point I emphasize is that one is always in control during the hypnotic process. Also, that hypnosis is a naturally occurring state of mind. For example, we all experience trance state when we are daydreaming, engrossed in a good novel, play or movie, or perhaps experiencing 'highway hypnosis' when driving long distances. We shut out the external world and get lost in our reverie.

As we relax deeply, the critical factor of the mind is set aside so that we can focus deeply on the healing suggestions. Hypnosis is a very subtle tool. It works by changing attitudes, beliefs, habits and perceptions. Throughout the years as I have worked with clients, I realized the truth and peace within was buried beneath layers of anger, hurt, judgment, resentment and past negative experiences. When we go within during hypnosis, we are accessing the unconscious mind and guiding it to remove blocks, thus beginning to build upon beautiful strengths, resources and capabilities that were within all along. Each of us has this power to heal and to access this inner wisdom, knowledge and ability.

In addition, just fifteen minutes of hypnosis is equivalent to one hour of deep restful sleep. It is also a centering and grounding process. Furthermore, it increases the production of the neurotransmitter serotonin which is known as the 'feel good' chemical. Serotonin promotes relaxation, good sleep, increases memory and concentration as well as a sense of happiness and well-being.

When we are experiencing the hypnotic state, we are journeying within to a process of self-discovery. Step by step we release those things that no longer serve us and keep us from achieving goals and being at peace. We are able to find that voice that relays to us the truth which lies within. As the inner and outer align, new possibilities begin to open up and life becomes filled with exciting possibilities.

Initially, as we communicate with the unconscious mind, we begin to connect to who we truly are, by recognizing our truth within. In essence, we begin to come home to self and align with this truth. This wisdom within is buried beneath layers of hurt, anger, resentment, old stories of who we were and what we think we can do. As we access the unconscious mind and help it to remove blocks, it enables us to climb higher and higher to achieve what we were meant to do and to become.

Through hypnosis, we tap into our deep connection to higher self, that part of us that is wise and knows our true path. We begin to realize that we are never alone, that the kingdom of the divine indeed lives within each and every one of us, providing what is needed is to tap into the consciousness of our true beauty and worth. As the mind is renewed during this initial stage and beyond with positive, uplifting thoughts, we align these thought patterns with the feelings of the heart and merge the two. This merging allows us to become balanced in mind, body and spirit.

During this initial stage of healing as we recognize we have a true self within, it is important to choose a different thought as we begin to align with that truth. Repeating a mantra or affirmation, helps to calm the mind, keeping it focused on something positive rather than running rampant with fear and anxiety. Stephen Covey in his bestselling book: "Seven Habits of Highly Effective People," says that affirmations are extremely helpful. He relays that this technique to reprogram the unconscious mind aligns us with purposes and principles that are important to us.

Incorporating affirmations into our daily lives will slowly help the mind to confront the disconnect between what we are saying in the positive statements and how we see ourselves. Repeating the affirmations helps retrain the mind to feel comfortable and ease when we are thinking in a positive way.

It is very beneficial to repeat each affirmation three times several times a day. Also, doing so at bedtime reinforces these positive suggestions. If we choose to read the affirmations aloud, it is helpful to do so in a confident voice. To add more power to the positive affirmations, we can write each one down as we say it aloud. It is also helpful to post the affirmations in areas where we will see them often. For example, we can place the affirmations on a sticky note on our desk, drawer, mirror, nightstand, refrigerator, car dashboard or computer monitor. We can also slip it into our wallet or carry a small notebook with us.

In addition, it is helpful to look at ourselves directly in the mirror and say each affirmation aloud during this time. The unconscious mind learns through repetition, so repeating the affirmation while doing this 'mirror work' is very powerful. If mirror work resonates, the book: "Mirror Work," by Louise Hay can be very helpful.

Also, it takes daily repetition of positive affirmations for the old negative programming to let go. It usually takes approximately eight to twelve weeks for permanent change to occur. So please stay with the daily affirmations for that length of time before moving on to the next set of affirmations given in the succeeding chapter. Once again, the old negative programming will begin to lose its grip on the unconscious mind with the daily practice of affirmations. Most individuals see a difference within the first week or two, however, it does take eight to twelve weeks for permanent change. It's important that we're very patient with ourselves during the process, giving ourselves a lot of credit for even the most subtle of changes. For this means the affirmations are taking root and beginning to grow and flourish.

For example, the following affirmations are very beneficial in reducing stress and beginning to connect to the truth within.

Please say each one three times:
1. "I am at peace with myself and with the universe."
2. "I am now easily allowing any outside stress to dissolve and fade away."

3. "I am more relaxed each day and this allows me to heal and connect to my true self."

In addition, the following two techniques can be done in the midst of any busy day. They are a quick and effective way to center and ground ourselves; bringing forth a sense of calmness and peacefulness. These techniques will begin to help us become balanced in mind/body and spirit, as we begin this journey to align with the true self.

The first is called 'Cook's Hookups' and is very beneficial. This a touch for healing technique which is very calming. We can do this at work, during class, right before a big test or presentation or anytime it may be needed. This method slows down an overactive left brain and brings and overactive right brain into focus. First, cross one ankle over the other and cross one wrist over the other (with the same side ankle and wrist on top); place tongue on roof of the mouth, just behind teeth and breathe deeply for thirty to sixty seconds. After this time has passed, uncross the legs, place all fingertips together and breathe deeply.

The other relaxation technique is 'Emotional Stress Release'. This technique not only reduces stress but helps our mind respond to outer events and inner thoughts differently, it also brings us back to being 'at choice'. This method is done by lightly holding our forehead and back of the neck; closing our eyes and focusing on our breathing for thirty to sixty seconds. Initially, as we are learning these techniques, we can always remember this quick way to reduce stress. Simply hold the forehead and back of the neck and breathe slowly and deeply for approximately one minute. This is a very beneficial and easy technique to recall as we are learning the various ways to reduce stress and reconnect to the truth of who we are. Bringing us back to a sense of being at choice as the true self can begin to generate creative solutions to the situation at hand.

Once again, through my experience, I have found the first stage in healing from anxiety, stress or any challenging issue, is the recognition of the true self within. To make our lives more consistent with the aspirations of being calm, relaxed, and peaceful, we have to start by knowing who we really are and not what we think we are, not what we wish to be, or not what we feel we *should* be. Then we will know what needs to be changed, what needs to be released and given more emphasis so that we can see more clearly what we want to be, and the way we want to live.

Disidentification, the capacity to observe self, is a wonderful tool and practice that can connect us to our true selves. When we are totally identified with our thoughts, feelings or actions, and believe that is all we are; then we become the impermanent circumstances in our lives. However, when we observe our thoughts, feelings, reactions and ways of doing things, we learn to see clearly who we truly are. We see ourselves as human beings who are experiencing anxiety not with the identification, 'I am anxious'. Thoughts, feelings, actions, and judgments are passing experiences of our self. Disidentification helps us to see them as passing and relative so we don't attach or cling to them. We learn that our thoughts, feelings, actions, and judgments are not part of our true selves. They are transient and are temporary experiences. In time we learn that all is temporary, it all passes through if we do not identify, attach, cling or obsess over these experiences.

We can practice disidentification by remembering that

we are not just the thought or feeling that we are experiencing at the moment. The following disidentification process is a powerful way to touch on thoughts, feelings, actions and judgments without identifying with them so we do not create symptoms of anxiety, stress or panic. In this way, disidentification leads to the connection to the true self. By separating ourselves from feelings, thoughts, and reactions which are passing and temporary, we become centered in our true selves. This aspect of ourselves which never changes, is always wise, peaceful, forgiving, unconditionally loving, and creative. We then open ourselves to life with a new awareness and understanding. Disidentification helps us to know ourselves as we truly are, and to remain connected to the level of spirit consciousness, expanding our sense of self.

The following disidentification process is very helpful anytime we wish to center and ground in our true selves. It is especially helpful when we feel we are ruminating or obsessing over negative thoughts, feelings, actions, or judgments. The mind learns through repetition, so the more we engage in this exercise, the more it is integrated and brought forth in our daily lives, helping us to shift out of anxious thoughts and feelings more and more easily as we come home to our true selves. This process is based on the work by Roberto Assagioli as cited in the book; "The Soul of Psychosynthesis: The Seven Core Concepts" by Piero Ferrucci.

Disidentification Process:

Allow yourself to experience these following words as your own thoughts, and as you hear these words within yourself, you will begin to experience what is suggested here.

I have a body, but I am not my body. My body may find itself in different conditions of health or sickness, it may be rested or tired, but that has nothing to do with myself, my real self. I may even have the desire to do something, but recognize that my body is not able to participate. I value my body as my precious instrument of experience and of action in the outer world, but it is only an instrument. I treat it well, I seek to keep it in good health, but it is not myself.

I have body, but I am not my body.

Focus your attention on this central thought here: "I have a body, but I am not my body." Attempt, as much as you can, to realize this as an experienced fact in your consciousness. How you have a body, but you are not your body, you are s/he who is aware of having a body.

I have emotions, but I am not my emotions. My emotions are varied, frequently changing, and sometimes contradictory. They may swing from love to hatred, from calm to anger, from joy to sorrow, and yet my essence ---my true nature --- does not change. "I" remain. Though a wave of anger may temporarily arise within me, I know that it will pass in time; therefore I am not this anger or any other emotion that may arise. Since I can observe and understand my emotions, and then gradually learn to direct, utilize, and integrate them harmoniously, it is clear that my emotions are not myself.

I am aware of having emotions, but I am not my emotions.

Focus your attention on the central thought here: "I have emotions, but I am not my emotions." Attempt as much as you can, to realize this as an experienced fact in your consciousness. How you have emotions, but you are not the emotions that arise within you; you are s/he who is aware of having an emotional experience. You are the experiencer of the emotion, not the emotion itself.

I have desires but I am not my desires. My desires are aroused by my drives, whether physical or emotional and by other influences. They are often changeable and contradictory, with alternations of attraction and repulsion; therefore they are not me. I have noticed how a desire once met ceases to be as attractive as it was before I responded to it. The first taste of my favorite dessert is not as satisfying as the one hundredth consecutive bite. I can realize that I have desires, but I am not my desires.

I have desires but I am not my desires.

Focus your attention on the central thought here; "I have desires, but I am not my desires." Attempt as much as you can to realize this as an experienced fact in your consciousness. How you have desires. but you are not the desires that arise within you; You are s/he who is aware of the desire arising within you that you can choose to respond to or not. You are the experiencer of the desire, not the desire itself.

I have a mind, but I am not my mind. My mind is a valuable tool of discovery and expression, but it is not the essence of my being. Its contents are constantly changing as it embraces new ideas, knowledge, and experience. Sometimes it refuses to obey me. Therefore, it cannot be me, myself. It is an organ of knowledge in regard to both the outer and the inner worlds, but it is not me.

I have a mind, but I am not my mind.

Focus your attention on the central thought here: "I

have a mind, but I am not my mind." Attempt as much as you can to realize this as an experienced fact in your consciousness. How you have thoughts, but you are not the thoughts that arise within you; you are s/he who is aware of the thoughts arising within your awareness that you can choose to identify with or respond to or not. You are the experiencer of your mental activity, not the thoughts themselves.

I engage in various activities and play many roles in life. I must play these roles and I willingly play them as well as possible, be it the role of child or parent, wife or husband, teacher or student, artist, craftsman, technician, sales representative or manager. But I am more than the child of someone, the parent, the spouse or partner, the worker or the professional. These are roles, specific but partial roles which I myself am playing agree to play and can watch and observe myself playing.

Therefore, I am not any of them. I am self-identified, and I am not only the actor but the director of the acting.

I have many roles in my life that I play, but I am not any of these roles.

Focus your attention on the central thought here: "I have many roles in my life that I play but I am not any of these roles." Attempt, as much as you can, to realize this as an experienced fact in your consciousness. How you participate in many activities and play many roles but you are not the roles that you perform; you are s/he who is aware of these roles and activities that you perform but you are the actor not the role you are playing and do not have to identify with that role. You are the director of the roles you play, not the roles themselves.

Next comes the phase of identification:

What am I then? What remains after having disidentified from my body, my sensations, my feelings, my desires, my mind, and my actions? It is the essence of myself --- a center of pure self-consciousness. It is the permanent factor in the ever-varying flow of my personal life. It is that which gives me a sense of being, of permanence and its energy. I recognize and affirm myself as a center of pure self-awareness and of creative, dynamic energy. I realize that from this center of true identity I can learn to observe, direct, and harmonize all the psychological processes and the physical body. I choose to achieve a constant awareness of this fact in the midst of my everyday life, and to use it to help me and give increasing meaning and direction to my life.

Focus your attention on the central realization: "I am a center of pure self-consciousness and of will." Attempt as much as you can, to realize this as an experienced fact in your awareness.

I would also like to include this short visualization to help readers begin to connect to their true self/higher selves. You may wish to record the visualization on the voice feature memo on your phone or other device. Find a quiet, comfortable place to sit or lie down, close your eyes and begin breathing in deeply and exhaling slowly five times.

You may wish to set a timer for the visualization for at least fifteen minutes or longer if you wish. The unconscious mind cannot tell the difference between a visualization and an actual event. For example, studies at Stanford

University showed, via PET scans, that regions of the brain lit up exactly the same way if a person saw the color red or thought of the color red. Thus visualizations are effective whether one believes in them or not. However, they will work faster and more effectively when you believe in them.

When using a visualization, bring in as many of the five senses as you can. Make it as detailed as possible. Please use this visualization each time you feel anxiety, stress or worry. It becomes more effective with use. You may prefer to think of imagining rather than visualizing if that is easier for you. Visualizations are powerful, proven techniques for refining your self-image and making important changes in your life. When you visualize positive, healthy changes, you begin to manifest them into your life.

The following visualization will help you begin to connect to your higher self/true self and reduce anxiety, stress and worry. Please close your eyes and take five long, slow deep breaths. Then see/imagine or visualize your higher self as a beam of white light going to that place in your body that feels anxious, stressed or worried. Often this will be the solar plexus region (in the middle of your trunk right below the center of your rib cage) or the 'pit' of your stomach. Let that area be filled with Light until the anxiety dissolves or fades away.

Keep directing the white light from your higher self to that region until it completely settles down and is free of anxiety. In this way, you are bringing the essence of your true self to the feelings of anxiety and stress. As you continue to use this visualization, you are making contact with your true self by beginning to forge that relationship, knowing that you are never alone. Your true self is always with you, helping you to shift out of anxiety more and more easily. Aligning you with the peace which is always at the core of your true self.

I would like to conclude this chapter with a meditation for readers on recognizing the truth that lies within you:

Some beneficial helpful tips on using the meditations include reading the meditations aloud as you record them on the voice memo feature on your phone. If you choose to do this, please read the words slowly and calmly. Playing soothing music in the background helps the mind to relax.

Find a quiet, comfortable place to sit or lie down, close your eyes and breathe in deeply and exhale slowly five times prior to listening to the meditation. Listening to the meditation at least once a week is very beneficial. Stay with whatever arises. When thoughts or feelings arise, stay with them and allow the words of the guided meditation to carry you through. Don't worry about clearing the mind. If thoughts come as you listen to the meditation, just let them come and then let them go as if they are birds or clouds passing through. Finally, develop a loving attitude. When you note thoughts and feelings arising during a guided meditation, look at them with a loving, friendly attitude. They are part of you and are coming up for understanding and healing. Allow the process without judgment.

Please close your eyes and begin to breathe deeply and slowly five times.

Imagine yourself in a peaceful place, anyplace you wish. It could at a beach with a fresh breeze blowing, a mountain area with a lake and clean, fresh air, a beautiful garden, a place you have visited or one in your imagination. All things are possible in this private, peaceful place… let's take a walk out of your peaceful sanctuary and onto a small path. You feel more peaceful and comfortable with each step you take on this path... feeling so safe, secure and comfortable... this path leads you to reconnect to the deep wellsprings of calm within you.

As you walk along this path you notice the trees... you may hear a bird sing... see the sunlight filtering through the trees... there is a warm, gentle breeze blowing softly... feel the warmth on your skin... and as you casually walk you see beautiful flowers of various kinds. In magnificent colors you have never seen before... it is all so peaceful and beautiful... and as you continue on the path... you come upon an ancient brick labyrinth... a sacred path to health, wholeness, the truth within... you notice stone benches scattered around to provide a place for reflection... you move toward one of the benches... you sit down comfortably.

You begin to reflect as you prepare to enter the labyrinth... prepare to meet and discover your true inner being... (you may pause for as long needed). You are now ready to enter the labyrinth and as you rise you feel a lovely breeze... gently moving you toward the beginning of this path... a path which leads to the center and out again... and so as you enter the labyrinth, you release all cares, concerns, worries, burdens... the path winds throughout and becomes a mirror for where you are in your life... walking into it with an open mind and an open heart.

As you reach the center... you receive a message that leads you to leave those outdated patterns behind you and deepen your faith in yourself... stay there as long as needed until the communication is complete for now... for in this stillness and silence you have gifted yourself... you realize that the spirit and heart long to just be in the stillness... to hear the truth within... the truth that the soul wishes to convey... simply being in this moment of stillness and healing allows the heart to open to what spirit wishes to convey to it... to guide you gently on your next step... in this moment... you are recalibrat-

*ing and adjusting self… furthering and advancing understanding…
that you are leading from the heart center rather than with the mind.*

*Your mind grasps immediately what an experience appears to
be… but it is the interpretation of the heart that leads you to understand
how you feel about that experience… the truth within the heart
would ask you to stop and open your heart to a moment of joy…
whenever and as often as possible… recognizing the truth that quiet is
required by the physical, emotional and mental bodies… take a few
moments to absorb this information and transformation.*

When you are ready, simply open your eyes and you are
back in a wide, awake fully alert state feeling balanced in
mind, body and Spirit.

I will share additional, helpful techniques to ground,
center and calm oneself in the chapters that follow. As well
as providing further visualizations and meditations to help
the inner and outer align in this process of self-discovery
and healing.

CHAPTER TWO

"Creating a Healing Space"

"I am safe and secure in my sacred healing space."
"I am one with my higher self."
"I am one with the universe."

During the next phase of healing, we begin to create a healing space we can return to again and again. The unconscious mind begins to create this safe, sacred sanctuary for self as we begin to heal.

In this fast-paced world, it has become essential for us to discover ways to relieve stress and create a calm, healing space within. I have seen an increase in the number of clients who are experiencing anxiety and stress related issues. I could easily empathize with their struggle as I too at times would become overwhelmed and overloaded by the demands of everyday life. Through my experience with hypnosis, I understood the great benefit of going within during times of anxiety, stress, upset, and frustration.

Once again, there are many benefits arising from the hypnotic state. As we learned previously, just fifteen minutes of hypnosis is equivalent to one hour of deep restful sleep. It is also a centering and grounding process, and increases the production of the neurotransmitter serotonin. Serotonin is the feel-good chemical that promotes feelings of well-being, safety, security and happiness. It also promotes sound restful sleep and increased concentration and memory.

Because of these incredible healing benefits, I practice self-hypnosis each day and share the importance of doing so with my clients. There are many ways to practice self-hypnosis, most of my clients find it easiest to listen to a guided hypnosis CD. With each client, I provide various CDs as we move along during the healing process. We work together to help home in on what comes up for them in between sessions. In this way, they can turn to the recording that most resonates with them at that time. They can create the healing space that is most beneficial for whatever issues are arising for them in that moment.

Others practice self-hypnosis through using a method learned during our session work. Though there are many ways to practice self-hypnosis, I believe the following method is an effective one. The practice begins by finding a quiet place where you will not be disturbed. First, repeat three positive affirmations, saying each one three times.

For example, you could say the healing affirmations which are in alignment with creating a healing space within: "I am safe and secure in my sacred healing space."

"I am one with my higher self."

"I am one with the Universe."

After reading each affirmation three times, sit or lie

down in a comfortable position and close your eyes. Inhale deeply and exhale slowly five times. Raise your index finger on either hand, and then bring it down slowly. Count backwards from five to one.

Put your thumb and index finger together and just allow yourself to relax. Say to yourself, *I am completely relaxed.* Remain in this state for at least fifteen minutes, while in this state of relaxation you can see yourself calm and relaxed, easily able to cope with whatever may arise. See yourself with your new patterns of behavior. Hear yourself saying to others how the new, positive behavior is working in your life. Allow yourself to the feel the difference as you achieve the goal you set for yourself. At the end of fifteen minutes, you can count from one to five and on the count of five, open your eyes and be back in a wide awake fully alert state. Alternatively, you can simply set a timer for fifteen minutes.

The following are helpful tips to practice self-hypnosis:

1. Please practice your self-hypnosis daily. Remember, just fifteen minutes of hypnosis is equivalent to one hour of deep restful sleep. It is also a centering and grounding process as well as increasing the production of the neurotransmitter serotonin. This is known as the 'feel good' chemical which promotes feelings of safety, security and happiness. It also promotes sound restful sleep, decreases stress and increases memory and concentration.

2. You can practice your self-hypnosis in the morning; some people set their alarm fifteen minutes

earlier than usual in order to work in their practice. Alternatively, you may prefer to practice self-hypnosis prior to bedtime or at any time that is best for you. It is easier to incorporate the habit of self-hypnosis if it is practiced approximately the same time and place each day.

3. The key to success with your practice is to do self-hypnosis daily.

It takes daily repetition of healthy, positive affirmations given in self-hypnosis before the old programming lets go. Please be patient with yourself during this process. The old negative programming will let go as you practice self-hypnosis. It is very important to give yourself credit for even the most subtle of changes. This indicates that these changes are taking root and are beginning to grow and flourish in your life.

You may also choose to add the above self-hypnotic suggestions into a daily affirmation practice:

"I am safe and secure in my sacred healing space."

"I am one with my higher self."

"I am one with the universe."

Please remember to read each affirmation three times several times a day. Also, doing so before you go to bed. If you choose to read the affirmations aloud, please do so in a confident voice. Also, you may find it helpful to post your affirmations in areas where you will see them often.

Daily relaxation is extremely important. We accomplish twice as much when we are relaxed as we do when we are nervous, stressed and tense. According to Bernie Siegel (author of *Love, Medicine and Miracles*), "Meditation (and I would also say any trance state) *raises the pain threshold and reduces one's biological age. Its benefits are multiplied when combined with regular exercise."*

Once again, in the trance state the body elevates the production of the neurotransmitter serotonin. When present, serotonin creates feelings of well-being, relaxation, personal security and restful sleep. It helps the brain to be more focused and less distracted. Emotions such as joy, peace and happiness are usually triggered by normal or higher serotonin levels.

As we create this healing space within, we begin to take back control of our lives. We begin to see that no matter what may arise, we can go within and become centered, grounded and at ease. As we begin to utilize these new responses to tension and stress, our unconscious mind responds and brings this new way of being into our lives. We realize we can choose to be stressed, nervous or easily upset or we can choose to go within and create a space of peace, harmony and well-being. This new choice for peace and calmness in our lives begins to move throughout every part of our being. Becoming a permanent part of our personality and reality.

In this healing space, we can feel safe to feel all our feelings and feel safe to express our feelings. Getting in touch with who we really are and honoring our thoughts and emotions. An old adage relays, "What we resist, persists." Thus, it is so important to no longer resist negative thoughts and feelings. Allow them, sit with them, let them arise in this safe, healing space where no one can intrude and we can begin to get in touch with what is beneath the stress, anxiety, negativity. As we allow those thoughts and feelings to arise, they slowly become transformed as we go within.

As we continue to access this healing space, our mind creates a very special state of harmony, peace and security. We become aware of the fact that there is a part of our inner mind that is logical and rational. The unconscious levels of our mind can cooperate and understand so clearly and so reasonably that it can guide us wisely in all decisions we need to make.

The capability of the unconscious mind has been with us ever since our souls came into existence. Our mind has helped us in the past and it will continue to help us in the future.

Some people refer to this part of the mind as their inner guide or inner advisor. Regardless of the name we call it, it has the special function of guiding us from within. It protects us and works out solutions to problems. This unconscious level of our mind helps us develop confidence in ourselves. It has its own way of helping us learn the difference between the past and the present.

It allows us to remember what we need to remember about the past and stores away information our mind feels is unimportant at the present time.

However, once we do remember, we understand that we do not need to be what those unpleasant past memories represent. Our inner mind recognizes we can be free from the past. We can live a much happier, healthier, more enjoyable life now and in the future. We can be aware of the fact that every day, in every way, we continue to become better, physically, mentally, emotionally and spiritually.

We continue becoming stronger, wiser and healthier.

Our understanding of life continues improving. We realize more and more that we are fulfilling God's purpose in our own special way.

As we recognize the truth within us and return to this healing space, we begin to achieve amazing accomplishments. At the same time, we achieve a very special balance between our time for work and our time for recreation. Between time given to others and time for self.

By doing this, we learn to accept ourselves as a good and special people. We respect our thinking, our feelings, our emotions, and develop a sense of pride and self-worth.

As we continue to advance and progress, we develop greater confidence in ourselves. We view ourselves in a wonderful way. Beginning to have a growing confidence in our talents, our skills, our attitudes and our abilities.

While in this healing space, our inner mind will continue to guide us just like an internal coach. Even while asleep at night, our minds will be working, causing our mental abilities, our physical abilities and our creative abilities to keep emerging more and more.

This will continue on a daily basis throughout our lives. The more confidence we develop as we go within and trust what we find, the more successful we become in all aspects of our lives. Our belief in ourselves will continue to increase each day and we will develop a confidence in our ability to reach our goals.

In this healing space, we create an appreciation and enjoyment for life. Developing a sense of peace with ourselves and with the world. As we return to this healing sanctuary within, our minds and bodies become relaxed, calm, and more at peace with the universe.

Each day our minds will become clearer and more alert which creates the ability to make wise, well-thought out decisions. It also develops the ability to organize our time and energy and always put everything in the right perspective. We begin to move ahead with confidence, knowing that each decision we make is the right one for us.

During the time I juggled my graduate work with raising a family, I discovered the great importance of finding time daily to go within. I used the practice of self-hypnosis each day. This is a practice I continue to do daily all these years later.

The feelings of being overwhelmed and overloaded with life's demands are ones that many women share. When I took those fifteen minutes to go to my healing space within, I emerged feeling centered and grounded. I am a 'people pleaser' and I began to notice that very gently my inner mind began to make changes. I found myself saying 'no' in a kind way to things that I knew would drain and overwhelm me.

Yet, it all unfolded in such a subtle manner that I still felt like myself. My inner mind led me to make these healthy changes in ways that felt very comfortable and safe for me. Putting up these healthy boundaries allowed me to balance my life in a healthy way while greatly reducing the feelings of anxiety and stress. I then had time and energy to have fun with my husband and children while balancing all my obligations. Healing ourselves benefits all around us.

A lovely client came to this realization when she felt utterly burnt out by the issues surrounding her adult children. Anna's children were very loving but, in her words, very needy. Though they were in their thirties, they would call her at all times of the day or night with any anxiety or worries they had. Anna's daughter was going through a divorce and her son had just suffered a devastating break-up with a young woman.

She dearly loved her children but was extremely overwhelmed by their demands on her time. In addition, she would worry about them constantly. We talked about the great importance of creating a healing space which she could return to in order to 'fill the well' so to speak. In addition, as Anna incorporated this knowledge and practice of self-hypnosis, she would be able to put up healthy boundaries. This would help her to regain her energy, balance and peace.

We began the session with the intention to create a healing space. Also, to be comfortable with putting up boundaries and bringing a balance into her life.

As Anna drifted deeply into the trance state, I asked her to set aside all worries, cares and concerns. To release any thoughts, any images except those which brought her peace and serenity. I relayed that she step into that sanctuary, that healing space. It was then suggested that she may find herself indoors or outdoors. Or perhaps, she may be in a space of feeling or knowing. Whatever was just right for her in that moment.

The session incorporated many suggestions about the ability and capacity she had to make a new choice. I also used regression work to go back to the very first time she felt the need to feel overly responsible for others. As we completed that work, it was suggested that from now on she come from a place of security, safety, love for self and others which always resides within. Her actions, behaviors, words and thoughts would continue to be filled with love, safety and security.

This was becoming a permanent part of her current identity, a permanent part of her personality and reality. These qualities had always been within, she only had been out of touch with them. Many suggestions were relayed to see how all that lives inside of her now. Because they did reside within, this realization allowed her to tap into these qualities and bring them forth as needed. How it is all reflected around her, in every part of her life, each and every day.

Because Anna had a great affinity with the Angels, I suggested that in her quiet times she should become more and more connected to her angels and their support. She was guided to feel that love and safety within her, anchored into every cell. That this inspired connection was available to her always from that moment on. So, she could then come from this place, this healing, sacred place, anytime she had to deal with her children, other loved ones, or any and all people. That this healing place within influences all her actions, words, her behaviors and all aspects of her life.

When Anna emerged from the session, she had tears in her eyes. She said she was in the most beautiful place, in Aruba with her husband. She felt the sandy beach, the warmth of the sun on her skin and the loving, presence of her husband next to her. The client also relayed that during our regression work she immediately saw her mother and because her father had issues with alcohol, she felt overly responsible for mother. She felt responsible for her mother's happiness and safety. Anna had felt this way since she was a very young child. Her unconscious mind had relayed this to me in hypnosis and with specific suggestions for healing during our session, she forgave her parents and rescued her little girl and promised the little girl they would bring balance, peace, boundaries and self-love into their intertwined life.

Anna recounted what occurred during our session and said it was so beautiful because at that moment, she felt angelic support all around her. In the angelic presence, she felt filled with all that love, support and security. Anna could feel it flowing into the very core of who she was. She felt the angels washing away anything that did not match with this vibration, a vibration that reflects perfect safety, security and love.

At that point, Anna described how she then returned to the beautiful beach in Aruba. She said, "I can return there anytime I want to! That is my healing space!" At the next session, she described how her son had left a long voicemail at approximately one in the morning. She listened to it and knew he was safe, just upset about the breakup. As opposed to calling him the next day, Anna texted back with a very short message. She was so proud and happy that she was able to set and keep a healthy boundary.

She continued to put these boundaries in place, loving and being there for her children and others without an over sense of responsibility and the resulting feelings of anxiety, stress and fatigue. This all unfolded in a very gentle, subtle way. There were times Anna slipped into the old behavior, but it was so uncomfortable and draining that she would remind herself to keep the new behaviors in place.

She said she would take herself into her healing space, on that beautiful beach in Aruba and would fill herself with those feelings of peace, serenity and balance. Feeling an angelic presence all around her, supporting her and cheering her on in her healing progress.

Through my experience, I view the healing process as a dance. We take steps forward and there may be times we step back a bit; loving ourselves, having great compassion for ourselves on the healing journey. Also giving ourselves a lot of credit and acknowledgement for even the smallest steps forward. During the healing process, it is very normal to do this 'dance'; to pass from one stage of healing and slipping back into an earlier stage before progressing to the next. We do not develop mastery and healing all at once. Healing is a process and it is very important to honor that process.

I offer my clients my support and also great respect for where they are in their healing journey. Throughout our work together, I remind them of how far they have come and how we all rise and fall back a bit and rise again as we gain mastery along the healing way, knowing we are reaching our healing goal slowly, gently and lovingly. It is a cycle of progress that grows stronger as each day passes.

Whenever I think of the 'dance' in healing, I often recall an amazing young woman I had the privilege to see in my practice. Eve had multiple phobias which prevented her from enjoying her life. These issues prevented her from spending the night with a friend, joining a school club, learning to drive, babysitting, and flying to see her grandparents who lived in Florida.

She gently, slowly made and maintained much healing progress as we worked together. Gradually, Eve began to spend the night with various friends from school, began driving lessons, and baby sat regularly. Approximately one year after working together, she calmly told me how we needed to reschedule our monthly session because she was flying to Florida to see her grandparents! I expressed how proud I was of her and recounted her many gains in healing, relaying that she had done all the work, it was inside of her all along.

She courageously committed to releasing all that no longer served her, reaching in and connecting with her many resources, strengths, capacities and capabilities. How she connected to the truth and the beauty of her true identity . She said she couldn't believe it had all happened so gradually and subtly. Eve relayed she felt so safe making the changes and trusted that as she moved forward and slipped back that she would eventually overcome those issues. Later that day, I received a phone call from her mother. Her mother relayed that her daughter burst into tears of joy as she recounted how far she had come. Eve said hadn't realized how much she had changed, how much her life had changed and was so very grateful for all the healing.

I cherish and treasure a beautiful graduation photo and note she sent to me. It always reminds me not only of this incredible young woman, but how many times the healing unfolds in this series of gentle, steps, unwinding and transcending all that held us back and down, until one day we realize that great truth within us. We have connected to our true self and all the gifts and treasures that lie within.

When we allow ourselves that time to return to our safe inner sanctuary, we 'refill the well' so to speak. We become more calm, relaxed and more at peace with ourselves, our loved ones and the world around us, bringing forth these treasures which lie within into every aspect of our daily life in ways that are very safe, appropriate and healing for us.

In addition to the self-hypnosis practice, the following is a visualization to help readers create their healing space:

Close your eyes and begin breathing in deeply and slowly five times. Now count backwards slowly from five to one. When you reach the count of one, slowly raise your right index finger and say to yourself, *I am deeply relaxed*. As you reach this state of complete relaxation, you enter your own private haven. A beautiful place of peace, comfort and serenity. A place where you are deeply relaxed, a healing place where it's safe to feel all your feelings, a place where it's safe to express your feelings, a place where you are safe, relaxed and at peace.

And now, allow your unconscious mind to open fully as a flower opens to the rays of the sun. Listen to the relaxing sounds all around you, become aware of your own easy breathing. Feel the relaxation flowing through your body and visualize yourself relaxed and at peace in this beautiful place. (pause) As you look around in your mind, you may find yourself indoors or outdoors or you may find yourself in a healing space of feelings and knowing, whatever is appropriate for you.

Now imagine a room in your mind. This room contains a switch that turns off or slows down your thoughts. Take a moment to locate your switch and when you are ready, turn it off. (pause) Notice how quiet and serene it is in your mind now. This switch may be turned back on whenever you wish. But, for now, you may prefer to leave it off for short while. Whenever you are ready, simply open your eyes and you are back in a wide, awake fully alert state knowing you can return to your healing space whenever you wish.

May the following mediation also help you to reinforce, create and strengthen the healing space within. You may wish to set a timer to emerge from the meditative state of simply count from one to five and on the count of five telling yourself you are back in a wide awake, fully alert state.

Please close your eyes and begin to breathe deeply and slowly five times, then imagine a peaceful place, anyplace you wish. It could be a beach with a fresh breeze blowing, a mountain with a lake and clean fresh air, a beautiful garden, a place you have visited or one in your imagination. All things are possible in this private, peaceful place.

Now as you relax even deeper in this safe place, notice how easy your breathing has become, a little slower and a little deeper too... and recognize how easily slow deep breathing alone can deepen a nice comfortable state of relaxation... every cell of your body becomes at ease as you continue to relax... and as you reach this state of complete relaxation, you enter your own private haven, a beautiful place of peace, comfort and tranquility, a place where you are deeply relaxed, a place where it is safe to feel all your feelings , a place where it is safe to express your feelings, a place where you are safe, relaxed and at peace.

Now allow your unconscious mind to open fully as a flower opens to the rays of the sun... and begin to count backwards slowly from ten to one, each descending number taking you deeper down, relaxed and at peace... on the number one you enter a beautiful place of peace and serenity... and so relaxing even deeper with... ten... deeper and deeper... nine... eight... seven... relax, relax, relax... six... five... halfway there now and when you reach the number one you are ten times more deeply relaxed than you are right now... four... three... two... and one... let the relaxation flow throughout your body and visualize yourself relaxed and at peace in this beautiful healing space.

It feels so good to be here... noticing if you are indoors or out-doors... are there any special sounds... any aroma... just allowing anything to come forward which would help create this space... since this is your sacred healing place... you can add or remove anything you want... take a moment to make this place perfect for you... this is your private, safe, sacred , healing space... relaxing here... letting go... relaxing just relaxing... everything is so peaceful and serene... continuing to drift... all is well... you are drifting with your own thoughts... and as you are drifting... you begin to drift away in your very own daydream.

Your conscious mind keeps relaxing more and more and your un-conscious mind and all levels of your inner mind are enjoying this peaceful place... you are drifting away in your day dream... and as you drift off you become aware of a soft gentle breeze... in this heal-ing, magical place you feel safe and secure... you see the light filtering down through the trees... the browns and greens of the trees... the ground beneath you soft and yielding... everything is so calm and peaceful... the following thoughts come to you... I am safe and sup-ported... I am serene and peaceful... I am creating a healing place within... a place I can return to at any time... here I find my deepest resources and strengths... I reach in and trust what I find... I bring it forth into every aspect of my daily life.

As you look up at the beautiful sky... you see the sun shining brightly... and its gentle soothing warmth shines down upon you... a golden ray of sun reaches toward you... gently... softly... soothingly... and you are enveloped in this comfortable warm ray of golden sunlight... you feel this ray of golden light pouring into your... through the top of your head... soothing and healing... it moves slowly throughout every part of your body... it flows through every organ... every system... every cell... every atom... every molecule... every muscle, ligament and tendon... throughout every part of you it flows soothing and healing... it removes from your body and mind... anything that no longer serves you... this ray of light moves throughout every part of you both seen and unseen... filled now with this wondrous, healing ray of light... and now the light moves around your body... protecting you from external stressors... any stress now just bounces off and away from this protective shield of light... which is invisible to anyone else... all positive loving emotions and thoughts, flow in and flow out from this shield of light... but it protects you from external stressors and external negativity... you are feeling safe and at ease... you now move through your daily life feeling very good... you feel safe, secure, protected because this beautiful healing ray of light has placed a protective shield around you... bringing this feeling forth into every aspect of your life... choosing this peace and calmness... knowing it is always your choice to call forth this shield around you.

Whenever your timer alerts you, you are back in a wide, awake, fully alert state, or whenever you count from one to five. On the count of five you are back in a wide awake fully alert state, feeling very good and knowing you can return to this healing space whenever you wish.

CHAPTER THREE

"Healing Through the Release of Anger and Resentment"

"All levels of my inner mind cooperate to resolve all conflicts in a loving way."
"I have a deep sense of peace within me."
"Every day in every way I continue becoming more kind and loving to myself and others."

In the next phase of the healing process, we discover the healing that comes through releasing anger and resentment. I have had the privilege of assisting my clients release longstanding issues surrounding anger, resentment, hurt and bitterness. Through the use of hypnosis, blocks are released which had prevented forgiveness of self and others. This leads to new levels of awareness, understanding and healing.

Through the years of working with clients, I realized that the healing and truth within was buried beneath layers of anger, hurt, resentment and bitterness. When we go within during hypnosis, we are accessing the unconscious mind and guiding it to remove blocks.

As we clear out these blocks, we are released from long-held feelings of anger and resentment. We are then able to release and forgive any people and situations from the past which have been unhelpful or unhealthy for us. We begin to understand that forgiveness has much more to do with ourselves than with anyone or anything we are forgiving. As we put past situations and negative experiences into perspective, we release their control over us. As we do this, we become aware of our power and freedom and the great courage which exists within each of us.

Though forgiveness is such a simple concept, it is many times very difficult to employ. Especially when working with clients who have experienced great trauma, I always emphasize that we are not condoning what happened. Forgiveness also doesn't mean needing to allow someone who has traumatically harmed us back into our lives or have a conversation with them. What it does mean is that we begin to take back power over our lives. We cease to be a puppet to the old outdated recordings that no longer serve us. As we honor and acknowledge what we have experienced, we then can let go of that which no longer serves us, allowing us to move forward in our lives in very powerful and positive ways.

Years ago, a client described being consumed with anger and rage toward her ex-husband. Felicia relayed they were married for eighteen years and he suddenly announced he wanted a divorce. This came as a shock because she felt they had a harmonious relationship. Felicia asked her husband why he wanted a divorce. He said he no longer was in love with her and would be moving out very shortly. He left their home within days and appeared indifferent and cold. Felicia began sessions with me shortly after the divorce was finalized, approximately one year after her husband left.

As we explored fully what transpired, she told me that the worst part was that he had lived a 'secret life'. Slowly, it was revealed to her that he had been having an affair for the last several years of their marriage. Also, he had been hiding financial accounts and other documents. When she confronted him, he admitted to the above without any remorse. He blamed her for his betrayal because he was jealous of her success and felt a distance from her, claiming that she boasted about her promotions and awards.

They both worked in the same field and she rose very quickly while he, unfortunately, did not. He took no responsibility for his actions and blamed Felicia for the demise of the marriage. Again, she relayed she was shocked because she felt they had a good relationship and felt she knew her husband. Through this traumatic time, she felt extremely hurt, betrayed, angry and enraged at what had transpired. Her husband refused to have in-depth conversations about the tattered relationship and was adamant about divorce.

When Felicia came to see me, she had been trying on her own to dissipate the anger and rage and move on with her life. Unfortunately, these negative emotions only intensified. As we explored all that had transpired, she said that not only felt betrayed by her husband but also by mutual friends and colleagues. She said that they were not supportive or understanding. As this continued, she felt an obsession to share with them all he had been hiding, to expose him and all he had done in secret. She thought if only people realized the truth about the man, she would receive the support needed.

As we worked together, Felicia realized that this obsession was only feeding the rage, hurt and anger. Through our discussions, she saw that she had family and other friends who were extremely supportive of her and understood the hurt and betrayal. In hypnosis, suggestions were given so that the unconscious mind would realize she did have great support, understanding and empathy during this very traumatic time. Slowly, it then allowed her to let go of the need to obsess and gain support from the above colleagues and certain friends. Further work was done due to regain a sense of self-trust. Felicia was very concerned that she had not seen the signs and was terrified this would happen to her again.

During one of our sessions, her higher self came forth and said that she had indeed seen the signs but blocked it out consciously. This occurred because she did not like conflict or confrontation. Higher self began to show Felicia scenes of times when she had noticed suspicious behavior on the part of her husband. She pushed this away, deep into the unconscious, because she did not want to deal with it. Also, scenes of her husband displaying jealousy was now evident to her in the trance state. Higher self, her true self, revealed that she was not to blame for her husband's jealousy. He had his own issues which did not allow him to express the truth and rawness of his own emotions. Instead, he chose to hurt her and to betray her.

After this session, we spoke about all that her true self revealed to her. Felicia said it was true that she did not like confrontation and avoided it at all costs. During future sessions, we helped the unconscious mind to feel comfortable with confronting unpleasant situations. Gradually, she began to feel safe in situations where there existed conflict. She felt safe in expressing herself calmly and confidently while allowing the other person to speak their truth. Slowly, Felicia regained self-trust. Trust that she would see signs of conflict in a relationship because she no longer feared it and pushed it away in her mind. As well as trust that she could handle and cope with any situation that may be unpleasant.

As her self-trust came forth, her anger began to dissipate, and she realized that she'd turned part of the anger toward herself for not allowing herself to see what had been transpiring. We continued to do work around releasing the long-held feelings of anger, resentment, bitterness and betrayal.

In one session, her higher self came forth again and showed her a marionette puppet. Felicia realized that by hanging on to the anger and unforgiveness she had unwittingly been pulled this way and that by her ex-husband. In this vision, the cords slowly released and set her free. She realized that forgiveness had much more to do with her than with her ex-husband. For by forgiving him, not *condoning*, but forgiving what transpired, he no longer held any power over her.

As she completely let go of the need to obsess over his betrayal, she took back her power. Felicia realized that through this difficult experience, she found her true self by discovering she had all the tools, resources and capabilities to handle any conflict and confrontation. Self-trust came forth as well as self-belief in all areas of her life.

As mentioned previously, the healing process can be likened to a 'dance.' We move forward a few steps and back again as our minds are learning new healthy patterned responses. As Felicia moved through this 'dance', layers emerged to be healed . Each layer stretching over a different, deeper emotion. One of the layers which emerged in order to be healed surrounded the need for outside validation. During the healing process, Felicia could see how the need to have her colleagues and certain friends validate her, only caused her more pain. She realized that it does not matter if someone validates an injustice done to her. After a trauma, it's far more important to release that need and learn to validate self. She realized that by needing other's validation, she gave her power away. By validating self, she slowly regained her power.

When anger came up, Felicia was more easily able to release it and regain a sense of control. We do need to allow angry feelings to come up and at that same time, explore what lies beneath the anger. We heal as we strengthen our connection to higher self and utilize techniques and tools to help move through anger, hurt and resentment. Not pushing away those feelings, but acknowledging, accepting and moving through them.

Through her sessions, Felicia learned to go to higher self for guidance where she found support, love, and wisdom, further confirming the importance of finding peace through connecting to our true self. As she gradually and completely let go of all those excessive negative thoughts and feelings, she released all that anxiety and stress, connecting to the part of herself that is clear, surefooted and at peace.

Unconscious memories, negative beliefs and experiences are very difficult to influence with the logic of the conscious mind. However, when we enter a hypnotic trance state when we are communicating directly with the unconscious mind and beginning to challenge those long-held negative beliefs and memories, we allow that part of self that was so hurt and wounded to finally be able to express itself.

That part had been holding on to all of that negative emotion, stuck in that past negative experience. As that wounded part is finally able to express all of its anger, hurt, fear, and resentment, it can finally let go and find a sense of peace.

During this time of healing, I have had the honor of witnessing clients release this great burden which they had been holding onto for many years. This healing is done in a very safe and gentle way. Slowly, gradually, those long-held negative beliefs and experiences are released and replaced with different thoughts and different feelings. Those based on self-love, self-worth, self-acceptance, self-respect and self-esteem.

As we validate what has occurred and all the feelings and thoughts that accompanied it, we can see how it is all just a collection of memories that no longer need to harm us in any way. During the hypnotic process, we are also accessing the higher self which resides in Spirit Consciousness, since the bridge from conscious mind to spirit consciousness is the unconscious mind. When that part of the mind is accessed, it helps us see and understand what has happened from higher point of view.

As we move into higher self, we detach and become the Observer. We can see that all we have experienced is an orchestration of events that helps us to grow and to learn. Even the most difficult situations bring us great lessons in growth and understanding. As with the above client, many times clients are extremely angry over injustices they have experienced. They cannot let go of the pain and hurt, and become bitter, frustrated and resentful.

This is especially true of clients who were bullied and treated unfairly by peers and others. The rage and anger toward these past instances of injustice consume them. The unconscious mind does not know the difference between the past and the present. In this level of the mind, time does not exist so the past and present are playing out simultaneously under conscious awareness. These past hurtful and painful experiences are there just beneath the surface triggering feelings of pain, outrage, bitterness and resentment.

When we go within during hypnosis, we are accessing the level of the mind that is holding onto this past, painful experiences. I ask the unconscious mind to go to the very first incident where something happened to cause these feelings of anger and resentment. As we access that memory, we bring in the adult reasoning mind to look at this very same situation from a different point of view, a more experienced, adult point of view. We can go back and change the past in order to heal the present and the future.

As the client relives that memory, I ask them to say what they have always wanted to say to that person or group of people. To see it as a movie and to edit the script any way they like for the most positive outcome. We allow as much time as needed to rewrite the script, allow it to play out, allow that part of self to express itself completely and fully. When that has been completed, I ask higher elf which exists in spirit consciousness to come forth. I ask higher self to please assist them to detox from the old anger, old negative emotions to exhale and with exhale blowing out all the old negative emotions connected to this issue.

As the client moves into spirit consciousness, they begin to let go of old painful memories, especially letting go of old unforgiveness in order to heal. Through my experience, I have seen that in these instances, higher self reveals that all was orchestrated in order to take back their power. Once they reframe the incident in the most positive way, with the most positive outcome, they have taken back their power, no longer allowing themselves to be a victim to past outdated recordings. As we continue with these healing sessions, they realize they are safe to free from all imprints of the past that are causing them anger and difficulty in this time of their lives.

It is a wonderful experience to witness these beloved souls empowered as they are freed from any negative control of past memories, events, beliefs, images or persons that had harmed them in any way. They are freed to be the happiest and most successful person they can be. Due to the release, reframing and learning that took place, the unconscious mind now knows and understands the person has the right to be healthy, happy and successful. They have a right to be freed from anything in the past that blocks them from reaching their goals and dreams. The inner mind understands that they deserve to be freed from these harmful past experiences.

When we can free ourselves of past negative experiences, we begin to experience a sense of inner peace and strength that relays to us an emotional healing is taking place. We then are free to choose to experience harmony in our lives. As we move from unconscious awareness to spirit consciousness, we realize that the higher self within enables us to overcome every obstacle we face. That we are special and unique and have a right to be happy and successful in all we do. Once we freely expect good things from life, life brings us good things. We begin to come from the understanding that all things are working for good in our lives. Each day brings new joy and healing into our lives and fills our souls with love and light. Releasing that past anger and taking back power over our own lives, encourages deep self–esteem, confidence and healing of the mind, body and spirit.

The power of love that comes forth from the healing of past anger and resentment brings harmony to all of our relationships. We become happy with what we are achieving for ourselves and grateful for the new life we are given. Healing from anger and resentment allows us to handle stressful situations more gracefully, with ease and confidence. We become more at peace with the Universe and at one with our own higher self, allowing us to find loving solutions to all problems. This enables us to be happier, healthier and more confident.

When we release these past negative, hurtful situations which resulted in long-held anger and resentment, we become happier with who we are. We realize we are the person that Universe wants us to be, becoming more and more aware that our live is received just as it is right now. Our past is approved, totally, regardless of whatever we did or didn't do. Regardless of whatever happened or didn't happen to us, we are free to move forward in our lives in the happiest and healthiest ways possible.

An individual kindly wrote to me describing what had taken place as she listened to the "Release Anger and Resentment" recording. She expressed eloquently how she had held on to longstanding hurts, resentments and bitterness. As she drifted into the trance state, she saw herself standing at the top of a mountain with a heavy backpack on her back. She was aware that the backpack contained all the heavy burdens of anger, resentment, bitterness, frustrations and all negative thoughts/feelings that had weighed her down.

She also became aware that she had the power within her to release these long-held negative memories and feelings. Her desire to become free yet retain any wisdom and learning from those experiences grew very strongly within her. In this moment of clarity, she threw the back pack over the mountain and saw it dissipate in a golden, white light. She became aware that she was free from the past and able to finally move forward in ways that were powerful, healthy and happy.

Some very beneficial techniques readers can utilize at this stage of healing include: Listening to a hypnotic CD on releasing anger and creating forgiveness. Also, utilizing your daily self-hypnosis while incorporating these following suggestions:

"All levels of my mind inner mind cooperate to resolve all

conflicts in a loving way"

"I have a deep sense of peace within me"

"Every day in every way I continue becoming more kind and loving to myself and others."

You may incorporate these same self-hypnotic suggestions into a daily affirmation practice. In addition, journaling can be helpful in order to express the anger and negative emotions that are coming up to be cleared. Everyone is unique, some really enjoy this practice of journaling and do so each day. Some prefer to do this once a week, others choose to do so only when experiencing anger and negativity. If you choose to journal, writing without censor is very cathartic.

While journaling, you may find the following suggestions to be helpful. Find a place that is free of distraction. You may write with pen and paper or prefer to type on a computer, whichever feels more comfortable to you. Begin by taking five slow deep breaths and close your eyes. Keeping your eyes closed allows your mind to communicate more easily without censoring what is coming out on the paper or screen.

You may also call on your higher self to come through and help during this process. Allow your hands to do what they want. Type, write or draw whatever comes into you mind. If you want a specific question answered, begin by writing down a question and allowing your hand to freely guide you to the answer. Don't try to interpret anything that is coming through, simply let your thoughts flow freely. When you feel finished with the session, take a few deep breaths to come back to yourself. Then look over what was written, hopefully something will come forth that is helpful.

This is a skill which takes practice, so in time the communication will come forth more strongly and more clearly. In addition, as was mentioned previously, utilizing the self-hypnosis is very helpful. For example, once you take yourself into the hypnotic trance state, see yourself standing before a celestial fire of enlightenment. This fire cannot harm you and as you watch the light coming from the flames you imagine seeing a powerful guide stepping forth.

This guide stands next to you , offering support as you toss into the celestial fire all resentments, hurts, anger, rage, injustices and other negative feelings As you see the smoke float into the sky, you feel a great sense of relief and release as you let those burdens go. Perhaps you may hear your guide giving you an important message about how to release anger and express anger in a healthy way.

Through the releasing of anger and resentment, we step into our power and strength. No longer allowing what has been to hold us down or hold us back. When we do not forgive, we are not only holding that person 'prisoner' we are holding ourselves prisoner. We take back our power and decide what person, situations or experiences will no longer be allowed to have a hold over us, allowing us to be free and reconnected to the part of us that is clear, sure footed and divinely motivated. Finding our power again allows us to step into our healing without delay and without hesitation on the healing path we are internally guided toward.

It is a profound experience to see the healing that comes about through the releasing of anger and resentment. I enjoy seeing these lovely souls begin to connect with the good experiences recorded in the unconscious mind as they are freed to move forward in their lives in very powerful and positive ways.

The following is a visualization which will help readers release feelings of anger, hurt, injustice, and resentment. Please close your eyes and take a slow, deep breath. Now place your hands over your heart. Send love and compassion to the part of yourself that is wounded and in pain. Ask your higher self to come forth and feel this support and love pouring down through you and surrounding you. Please move away from any thoughts about this hurt, anger, rage etc., and allow yourself to only feel it. Please move away from the head and drop into the heart completely and allow these negative feelings to come up in order to move them from the body. These emotions have been waiting to be expressed, healed and released. Each time you choose to use this healing visualization, this part of self finally feels heard and accepted. It will begin to clear, and you will feel more peaceful and ease as a result.

May this meditation help to release, and heal thoughts and feelings around anger and resentment:

Please close your eyes and begin breathing in deeply and slowly five times. You may set a timer to alert you at the end of this meditation or simply count from one to five and tell yourself that you are back in a wide awake, fully alert state. Allow yourself to relax even deeper, feeling so safe and so relaxed in your private haven. The purpose of this journey is to learn how to release anger and resentment, so that you may be free to move forward in your life. Free to discover your true self under the layers of anger and resentment.

Now, begin to focus on the chakra energy centers, starting with the first energy center at the base of your spine. The root chakra... please see or feel this beautiful red energy spinning clockwise like a wheel... and as it spins, any darkness falls away... Now just above the root chakra, seeing or feeling the sacral chakra... this incredible orange wheel of energy... spinning clockwise several inches above the root chakra... and as it spins, any darkness falls away and it becomes healthier and brighter... this vibrant, glowing orange energy.

Your attention now moves up the chakra center behind the navel... the solar plexus... your power center... a wheel spinning clockwise with its golden, yellow energy... as it spins... any darkness falls away... and it becomes healthier and brighter... your attention now ascends to your heart center... the heart chakra... seeing or feeling this energy center... spinning clockwise with its vibrant green energy... and as it spins, any darkness falls away and it becomes healthier and brighter... this vibrant green healthy energy... ascending now to the throat chakra... seeing, feeling or sensing a sky blue wheel of energy spinning clockwise... and as it spins... any darkness falls away... and it becomes healthier and brighter... this vibrant glowing sky blue energy.

Your focus continues to move up... the space between your eyes... your third eye... this chakra spins clockwise with a deep blue/purple energy... and as it spins, any darkness falls away and the third eye becomes healthier and brighter... this deep blue/purple energy... now ascending finally to the crown chakra... the energy center located inside the top of your head... and incredible violet color... spinning clockwise and as it spins all darkness falls away and it becomes healthier and brighter... an incredible violet color... your connection to the Divine... now feeling balanced and centered.

I wish you to see the night fall... to imagine yourself at night fall... standing in a wooded glen... safe, peaceful night... the sky above you dotted with beautiful stars... feeling more and more at peace... And you begin to see, feel or imagine a golden, white light descending from the sky moving into your crown chakra... and as it moves down... it pushes with it old harmful negative thoughts, feelings, emotions, experiences... pouring into all the places which held that negative energy... This golden light of the Universe is filling those spaces with joy, peace, unconditional love, self-trust and self-belief... watch as the beautiful light flows completely into your being.

As you continue to be cleansed and cleared by the golden white light... released, relieved, transformed... uncovering the beauty of your true self... free to receive whatever good and healthy things you want for yourself... free to recognize the truth within.

Whenever you are ready, simply count from one to five and on the count of five, open your eyes and you are back in a wide awake fully alert state feeling balanced in mind, body and spirit.

CHAPTER FOUR

"Nurturing the Inner Child"

"I am a worthwhile person."
"I feel confident and self-assured with everyone I meet."
"I deserve to be happy, playful and joyful."

In the first three chapters, we have focused on the healing that has come about through discovering the true self, creating a healing space, and releasing anger and resentment. Now we will discover the healing that comes about through nurturing and healing the inner child.

Through the use of hypnosis, one can reframe and release blocks that prevent the healing of childhood issues, leading to new levels of awareness, understanding and healing. Through my experience, I have found hypnosis to be a very effective and powerful tool in helping clients heal their inner child, thus transforming and empowering their lives in very powerful and effective ways.

When hurtful and traumatic childhood emotions remain unresolved, one remains frozen in the past, which negatively impacts one's life in the present. We may have heard the statement: "It is never too late to have a happy childhood." For we can "rescue" that injured child by going back through the various developmental stages and completing unfinished business. The unexpressed energy of that wounded child can be expressed and can be healed by working through the emotions that were not allowed to be expressed as a child. If one grows up in a dysfunctional family, they most likely learned to not express their emotions. However, it is never too late to express those emotions and heal old hurts, anger, trauma, and resentment.

Through the hypnotherapeutic process, we are asking the unconscious mind to review, assess, explore and bring in adult present understanding, experience and wisdom to reframe and release the negative childhood experiences and memories. As this healing occurs, the inner child becomes empowered and integrated into the adult self.

This healing allows the adult to create a 'clean slate', bringing in all the positive traits/attributes and goals they desire. As this healing process continues to unfold, one can begin to see their true beauty and worth, which was within all along. It is a joy to see clients healing their inner child who is the heart of who they are. Healing, accepting, and loving the inner child leads us to discover the child's gifts of joy, creativity, spontaneity, and lightness of being.

I have had the privilege and honor of helping many clients heal the wounded inner child. Many times a client will suffer from low self-esteem and confidence and will relay to me that no matter how much education, accolades, or accomplishments they have accumulated, they feel a deep sense of inferiority. They experience a continual lack of self-love, self-worth, self-value, self-acceptance and self-esteem. I recall one such example of a client who was extremely successful but constantly worried about being judged, criticized and felt inferior to others. As I looked over Joan's familial history, I could see the signs that her inner child had been greatly wounded. I suggested that we begin work on healing her inner child and she readily agreed.

During one of these sessions, Joan had a profound experience which led to the deep healing of her inner child. She realized how deeply injured her inner child had been. This led to the realization that she had denied how the dysfunctional experiences of her childhood had affected her. Joan had downplayed the enormous impact it had on her self-love, self-worth, self-acceptance, self-confidence and self-esteem. The blame had been turned inwards because she did not want to face nor believe the truth of those experiences and where the blame truly laid. Joan had chosen to believe that something was inherently wrong with her rather than believe that she had been emotionally and verbally mistreated. It was as though she was protecting the one who had mistreated her.

Through those hypnotherapy sessions, Joan was able to face the truth. Her inner child was finally able to express her pain, outrage and hurt over those painful experiences. As time went by, the anger and hurt of the inner child was also directed toward herself. For she had chosen to reject herself, not wanting to look at the past, denying the truth of those experiences. Through the session work, Joan was able to see this innocent child, embrace her and promise her that she would protect her from now on. A 're-nurturing' took place as she stood with her inner child as she was regressed to significant scenes in her past. In each of these scenes, the child was finally able to express her rage and hurt and as the adult she was able to help her reframe those events in order to back her power. Through the use of hypnosis, we are able to rewrite the past in order to heal the present and the future.

As the inner child healed more and more, Joan could forgive the one who had mistreated her. After multiple sessions, Joan found compassion and pity for that person for she realized the depth of his own pain and inability to summon the courage or capacity to face the truth of his actions. Also, the man didn't possess the ability to seek help in order to heal these deep-seated issues. As this occurred, Joan told me she truly felt reborn; feeling those painful emotional ties to the past severed. With her newfound power, Joan was no longer being a 'puppet', being pulled this way and that whenever she was triggered within. In fact, she ceased to be triggered by those old outdated memories and experiences. She threw off the label of victim and realized she was an ingenious survivor. All those painful experiences of the past transformed into wisdom, power and strength, no longer allowing the wounds of the past to hold her back or keep her stuck.

Joan also relayed to me she was actually grateful for those past experiences for they provided her with the ability to have great compassion and empathy for others who are in pain. During one session, Joan dialogued with her higher self which brought further healing and clarification of the childhood issues. Since the unconscious mind is the bridge from conscious mind to spirit consciousness, many times clients will access their wise higher self. The message her higher self relayed to her was so beautiful and profound I asked her permission to share it with others. Joan readily agreed and I promised to always protect her anonymity.

Her higher self began by relaying the following: "This part of you is the truth of who you really are. This had been an existence to love yourself, to value yourself, value and love self unconditionally. No longer judging self and we chose this existence because of the limits placed upon you as a child. The limited receptivity of who you really are. There had been very high expectations to live up to and very critical evaluations. Great burdens were placed upon your shoulders, too young to handle, so painful until you reached out for healing allowing yourself to be released from these self-imprisoned shackles. You sought out, 'we' arranged for this experience to play out perfectly. All played out as planned until we felt such burden that we began to strive to go within, to find our deepest resources and strengths and to teach ourselves. Wonderful abilities and strengths were there all along.

When you were tired of the weights placed upon you, you chose this process of healing to free yourself. Recognizing you could have resisted and stayed shackled by heavy weights. Thus, not finding our message of learning the greatest lesson of self-love. Instead, we overcame our deepest fears of not measuring up that held the lack of consciousness of our own beauty and worth. We began a difficult process of unleashing these shackles thus beginning to build beautiful blocks of golden light that enabled you to keep climbing higher and higher to achieve that which you were meant to do. Being able to erect a wall of golden steps leading you to wisdom and higher under-standing. Elevating the level of our being to serve as a glorious example and teach the many on your planet who came here to learn, to experience, self-worth, self-love, self-validation. For in doing so, one truly understands that loving self unconditionally is a process. Truly connect to all that is the essence of the Flame of the Light of the Heart of God.

To do what you have accomplished requires great courage. In the part of the journey to come, through this healing process, you will continue to release self from any last remnants of feelings of inadequacies. Look in the mirror, see the beauty and radiance of your true self looking back. Release the fear that still exists in personality self which is left, this is done through balance. Only the heart is of true value and worth. I thank you for releasing lingering fears held at subconscious levels, which is fear of wielding power wisely. You are afraid of abusing power, so part of your mission to accomplish here is to embrace your power. You will not abuse your power since this is only an issue with personality self. It is not in alignment which we know you hold in your Divine Self.

You can handle power easily and with great wisdom, since we know you keep pure intent in your heart of hearts. I wish to tell you it is a difficult tasking process, yet it can be cleared away as you are doing now by aligning thought patterns with the feelings of the heart and merging the two. The new thought patterns will undo and are in the process of releasing whatever is keeping you from loving self. Your heart radiates love from your being. We can easily pass this radiant feeling to others. See self encased in the golden white light of All That Is. Your true being, who are you not to reflect the Glory of God. You are beauty, Divine perfection, a being of light and love. Release self from having to do anything but shine and love and so it is, and I leave you surrounded with great love."

These words from higher self deeply resonated with Joan and as she emerged from hypnosis, she relayed how light and free she felt. She explained that as she moved through the various healing sessions, the mask she wore to hide her many fears, began to dissolve. Joan was able to transmute and transform the fears so she could become her true self, removing the illusions that had her back so that she could see clearly.

Another case study involved a woman who was beautiful, intelligent and successful in the business world. Outwardly, Sylvia's life seemed full and rewarding. Within, things were very different. Though she had reached many goals, feelings of depression and worthlessness plagued her. There were times she did not feel she could get out of bed in the morning and did not feel like engaging in activities that used to be pleasurable for her.

Sylvia had spent many years in psychotherapy and knew the origins of her feelings. Her earliest memories were of her mother's cruel behavior toward her. She was an only child and her mother would yell, scream and criticize her over the smallest matter. Her mother also belittled her constantly. She continually told Sylvia that she was a great disappointment.

Sylvia described being overweight as a child and her mother complained she could not find clothes to fit her. Within earshot of my client, she continually told others how she had to shop for her in a special section for plus sized children. Her mother continuously reinforced my client's feelings that she was worthless and deficient in many areas of her life.

Fortunately, at the age of twelve, Sylvia had a wonderful female teacher who saw her intelligence and true worth. During that year, they had long conversations about her family life. Her teacher helped Sylvia to see herself as worthwhile and to see her mother as a very flawed, deeply troubled person. Sylvia relayed that this teacher helped her to set goals and attributes much of her success to this wonderful relationship.

Yet, deep inside, the wounded child resided with residual feelings of shame and worthlessness. She sought hypnotherapy as a way to reach her inner child and release of herself from feelings of depression and worthlessness. During one of our sessions, she met her inner child at the age of seven. Sylvia talked with her, asking what she needed to heal. The child relayed to her that she needed and wanted to be acknowledged as a worthwhile person. She wanted to go outside and play. The client visualized taking her inner child outside to play, having long talks, reading her books and singing songs to her.

Through this process, Sylvia became the parent of her little girl. She treated her as she would have liked and deserved to be treated by her own mother. As Sylvia continued nurturing and loving her inner child, she felt a healing taking place. In one session she described the little girl climbing onto her lap and placing her arms around her. She realized she was the only one who could really understand what that little girl was feeling and needing.

Sylvia helped transform the inner child's feelings of loneliness, rejection and shame. Tears streamed down her face in one of our sessions as she held her little girl. Sylvia expressed to me post session that as she wept, she felt the release of the sadness of the past. As we continued to work together, she continued to release the layers of depression and shame. She was happier, felt worthy, deserving and had a deeper understanding not only of herself but of her mother's emotional problems.

Due to my own childhood issues, I recall being very concerned about the judgment of others. I was hypervigilant on a daily basis about how I looked, sounded, behaved and how others responded to me. Outwardly, I appeared calm but this turmoil always existed within. This negative belief system caused me much anxiety and stress, for I gave away my power to others to determine my self-worth. I allowed external circumstances to control how I felt internally. I had not yet discovered my true self. Thus, I had not discovered the ability to connect to my truth and true worth regardless of what was occurring externally. In my thirties, while in grad school, I was introduced to hypnosis course work. In the beginning chapter I described how it changed my life in powerful and effective ways.

During the hypnosis sessions in school, I became aware of this unconscious belief pattern. It had ruled my life for so long and had robbed me of my peace, self-love and self-esteem. This long held belief started to slowly unravel. The origins of this negative response pattern became evident. I was then able to rewrite the script so to speak. This allowed me to rewrite the past in order to heal the present and the future. The inner child finally expressed all she needed to say in a safe, loving, supportive environment. This brought about release, reframing and transformation. That part of self could forgive all involved, retaining all lessons and learning. Finally being free to move forward in positive and healthy ways.

Just as with my clients, I too moved through all the stages of discovering who I truly was. Initially becoming aware that I had a higher self, caused a huge shift in my healing. This awareness brought me such a sense of self-worth, self-love, self-trust and self-belief. It filled me with feelings of joy and hope.

More and more as I moved through this healing process, I understood on a profound level that I was a spiritual being having a human existence, which is true for each and everyone one of us. Creating the healing space, provided me with a safe place to delve deeply into the wounding and pain. Aligning with my higher self, allowed me to see all of these painful experiences from a vaster perspective, forgiving others for the roles they played and forgiving myself for believing what was never true about myself. This releasing provided me with the ability to bring in this vaster perspective through all the subsequent stages of healing.

As I released the layers of woundedness, healing the inner pain, I could see clearly how I no longer could give my power away. New healthy responses and neural pathways were created through repetition of daily hypnosis practice, affirmations, visualizations, tools and techniques. Healing is a process and gradually, I no longer became dependent on external circumstances to determine how I would feel about myself.

In the normal progression of healing, I moved forward

and back as I moved through this inner journey. Each time I came forward again, I felt stronger, wiser and more connected to my true self and to the Divine, no longer coming from a wounded place which created the need to be validated by others, or by external circumstances. Discovering my true self, releasing the unhealthy layers within, allowed me to see myself as worthy and deserving.

I had not realized how stressful and anxious I felt each day. I hid it well, but it was always there, bubbling underneath the surface. Through this healing process I could relax into life, trust life, and trust myself to cope with anything. Always, trusting in my true self/higher self to guide me wisely, felt just like I had an internal coach as well as trusting in Divine support and presence in every aspect of my life.

Once we begin to explore experiences of childhood abuse, neglect and pain, we may bring forth excessive feelings and thoughts causing us to feel overwhelmed. If this occurs, the most productive plan of action is to find a qualified therapist who can act as a guide or advisor. Qualified therapists who specialize in hypnotherapy can be found through the American Society of Clinical Hypnosis website: **www.asch.net**

Also, reading the following books may be very helpful: "Healing the Inner Child Within" by Charles L Whitfield, MD; "Your Inner Child of the Past" by W. Hugh Missildine and "Betrayal of Innocence" by Buck S. Fonvard.

Also, incorporating a daily self-hypnosis practice will greatly help readers to release negative patterns and anchor new ways of thinking and being. For example, you may wish to add the following affirmations to your self-hypnosis practice focused on healing the inner child:

1. "I am a worthwhile person."
2. "I feel confident and self -assured with everyone I meet."
3. "I deserve to be happy, playful and joyful."

You may also include the above self-hypnotic sugges-tions in your daily affirmation practice. It may be very helpful to the inner child to say these affirmations aloud in a clear and confident voice as you do 'mirror work.' Re-peating these affirmations confidently while looking into your eyes, will be very powerful.

In addition, the herbs chamomile, star anise and yarrow are appropriate during the healing of the inner child. Chamomile is used for love, protection and healing both in the bath or as a tea. Yarrow helps deal with negativity and star anise is used for negotiation between opposites. Also, the use of peppermint in your bath or as a tea could be helpful as it is good for protection. Thyme is identified with courage and ambition and enhances your ability to experience childlike fun. After a healing bath, you may wish to play a game you enjoyed as a child. Your inner child will be nourished also by lavender and rose fragranc-es. These fragrances are associated with love, protection, purification, balance and healing.

Please pick the fragrance that feels best and write a par-agraph about something from your child's experience that you wish to release. Light incense or add bath oil to a warm bath. Drop what you have written into a fireproof bowl and light it. As you take your bath, imagine those old memories dissolving in the scented water. Breathe through any emotions that may arise.

Cut a picture out of a magazine that your inner child may enjoy. Pick a place such as a playground or park or choose a toy that appeals to your inner child. Place this picture in a prominent place for at least one week.

Feel anxiety and stress continue to melt away as you get in touch with and heal your inner child. You may ask your higher self to help you work with your inner child. Creating and bringing in this help assists you in caring for this younger part. This work is very important because the inner child represents a part of self that has been rejected/ignored. When you reclaim this part, you will make peace with yourself in the process. Bringing about peace into all areas of your daily life.

The following is a wonderful way to help heal the inner child. This process is called "Meeting the Inner Child." For this therapeutic exercise, please close your eyes and take a deep breath. Allow your body to relax and surround yourself with a protective light, any color you wish. Imagine yourself in a beautiful outdoor sanctuary; perhaps a garden or meadow. At the edge of the meadow you discover a playground, it's a magical place. The ideal place to play outdoors. There you see your inner child. Notice what is this child doing? Is the child playing? Exploring? Or perhaps simply waiting for you.

Move closer to this child and notice how you feel. Tell this child that you are her/his adult self and that you have come to help the child heal. How does your child respond? Look into your child's eyes, what do you see? Talk to your child and tell your child your name. How does the child respond? Ask your child about her/his favorite food and favorite game. Ask your child what she/he fears the most and ask how you can help to relieve that fear. Find out how the child feels about you.

Take a few minutes to get acquainted. Let your child know you are there to help. Ask how you can help your inner child. When your child feels safe, see if you will be allowed to hold the child's hand or pick her/him up. Ask this child what they need from you. Explain that it is safe now to explore and learn about the world. Your child will not be judged, harmed or criticized ever again.

Bring your focus back to your breathing now. You have made contact with your inner child. It may take time for the child to trust you fully. Surround both of you with the child's favorite color. Take two deep breaths, focus on being in your body and bring your awareness back into the room.

Through accessing the unconscious mind and communicating with higher self in spirit consciousness, we can rescue the wounded inner child by regressing through various developmental stages and finishing the unfinished business. The unexpressed energy of that wounded child can now be expressed and healed by working through the emotions that were not allowed to be expressed as a child. We are able to rewrite and reframe the past in order to heal the present and the future. Doing so allows self to achieve what it desires and align these new positive thought patterns with the feelings of the heart in order to become balanced in mind, body and spirit.

May the following meditation support you, the reader, and your inner child in expressing, rewriting and reframing the past in order to heal the present and future:

Please close your eyes and begin breathing deeply and slowly five times. You may set a timer to alert you at the end of this meditation or simply count from one to five and tell yourself you are back in a wide away fully alert state.

As you drift deeper and deeper into your safe sanctuary, I would like you to imagine or sense a waterfall, a beautiful cascading waterfall, soft flowing waterfall in different and varying shades of blue. They are poured gently over you, very relaxing, very soothing, your heartbeat begins to gently calibrate to the rhythmic beating of the water gently cascading down. You are free of concentrating on your breathing, your body is naturally adjusting to the waters beat.

It's as if you and the water gently flowing are becoming one... it is pouring through you, releasing anything that has been held tightly... anything that has felt stressful... anything inside that has been constricting, that has been binding, any frenetic energies are just pouring away from you, are being washed out of you as if you are freeing yourself... as if you are becoming clearer, vibrating at your natural state, for water is always easy, gentle, free flowing, not bound nor constricted by time or schedules or demands, or expectations or limitations.

You are the water... you are washing yourself clear and clean and you are feeling more relaxed and freer then you have felt for a while... you are giving yourself permission to luxuriate in the feel of the cascading water... the gentle rhythm the heartbeat of life... you are clearing yourself as if you are a being reborn and working with a brand new slate free of old concerns or frustrations.

And now going to an inner place of journeying and imagine in your mind's eye because you are still near the waterfall... and beautiful beings of light, whatever you consider them to be... perhaps an angelic guide who has lovingly been with you for a long time... is reaching out to take your hand and you're agreeing to go with this beautiful angelic being wherever this being decides to go... for you will uncover what has been in shadow to shed more light on it.

You are now walking toward the waterfall and walking through the waterfall as if there were a chamber behind the waterfall that was not visible before... you literally glide through this doorway... your guide tells you that you have entered the cave, a cave-like structure of childhood... it is the cave or cavern of childhood where much has been recorded then left as you moved forward and grew larger and stepped out of this cave... though you may have worked on healing your inner child... there is still a crevice that you do not interpret as being monumental but merely a step on your accelerate path to healing... this is a crevice you can step into so you can view the experience of what that felt like in childhood.

You are now stepping, with the assistance of your Guide... into a crevice which contains a childhood memory which needs to be healed, cleared out... Let yourself go back in time as you count backwards from five to one... on the count of one, you are right there at a scene from your past... your unconscious mind knows exactly what memory to bring up... that's it... you are right there at that scene... imagine there is a screen in your mind just like in a movie theater... see your younger self on this screen... notice if you are indoors or outdoors... are you alone or with someone... it does not matter what scene is playing on your screen.

It may not even make sense at first... allow your scene to develop... just take your time... notice how old you are... as your scene takes form you may experience a time when perhaps you felt angry, hurt, sad, lonely, fearful, abandoned or ashamed... allow yourself to observe what is unfolding free from any judgments... remember you are not in this scene... you are observing it from a safe distance... as if you are in a movie theater watching a film... watch now and experience all the feeling associated with this event.

Take your time… from your current adult perspective notice what decision you made or opinion you formed as a result of this experience… did you form any belief about the world or about yourself after this event… I would like to invite your adult self and your guide to help you see this experience in a new way… rewrite this experience in the most powerful and helpful way… we will now give your child a voice, as the adult… lend your voice to this child and let your child yell, scream, cry or say whatever they have being waiting to say here in this safe protected place… where no one can intrude as the child expresses self and you as the adult self and guide all hold safe, sacred space for your child to finally be able to express the words and emotions your child has been holding for so long.

See the past attachment to this experience coming from your child as a ribbon from that event to the present… Your guide now cuts that ribbon so that the child is free to be with you, inside of you, healed and whole… now embracing your child and surrounding your child with unconditional love which is flowing from the Universe, from your guide and from your adult self… you have energetically rewritten this experience and also preserved all wisdom and learning from this experience… having and creating a new experience now.

Please press your thumb and first finger together on either hand and save these good feelings… from now on when your inner child wants to re-experience this good feeling, they can simply make that simple connection and their mind and body will be flooded with this positive change… that's it, stay with those good, positive and powerful feelings… bringing all those good feelings back with you as you begin to emerge from this meditative state… they are a permanent part of who you are now… a permanent part of your personality and reality.

Whenever you are ready, simply open your eyes, and you are now back in a wide, awake, fully alert state, feeling balanced in mind, body and spirit.

CHAPTER FIVE

"Learning Self-Love and Self-Acceptance"

"I am now loving and approving of myself."
"I am always feeling warm and loving toward myself."
**"I am easily able to maintain positive feelings about
myself in any situation."**

As we journey through this process and accept and love
the inner child, this leads to the next process of loving and
honoring self. Through the use of hypnosis, we can release
blocks that are preventing the experience and integration
of self-love, self-worth, and self-acceptance. This healing
leads one to new levels of awareness, perspective, and understanding. As we clear these blocks that were preventing
us from loving and accepting self, those previous negative
messages are cleared. We're then free to create new positive, healthy and loving messages. In other words, healing
allows us to create a 'clean slate' bringing in all the positive
traits/attributes/goals we desire. As this healing process
continues to unfold, we can begin to see and experience
our true beauty and worth, which has always existed within

self.

Learning to love ourselves builds inner strength and is the solution to suffering from issues on all levels in mind, body and spirit. It alleviates depression and enhances relationships. Even a slight opening in the door to self-love makes a difference. According to Gay Hendricks, psychologist and author of *Learning to Love Yourself Workbook,* "when we seek love without bathing ourselves in it from within, we will never be satisfied with what we get."

Nothing replaces learning to love ourselves. The following is a helpful tool for readers in learning to love self.

Please close your eyes for a moment and think of someone or something that you absolutely know that you love. It can be a person, place, a pet or anything at all. Notice the feeling in your body that accompanies those thoughts of love. What does the love feel like in your body? Where do you feel it? Notice how you experience this love. When you have a clear feeling of this love, shift that flow of love back to yourself. Imagine love flowing toward the person, place or thing then circle the love around them and bring it back to you.

If you lose the feeling, start again. If possibly the negative belief: "loving self is selfish" comes up for you, please place your hands over your heart and send love to the part of self that has having difficulty receiving love. Perhaps asking higher self to come in and bring wisdom to that part of self. As you send love to that part of self, please explain that loving self is not selfishness. For those who are truly selfish do not love themselves or others. They feel they are not enough and need to come from a place of selfishness. Also, loving self refills the well, so to speak. We cannot give to others fully if we are drained and exhausted.

As you utilize your daily self-hypnosis practice, bring in the affirmations I have listed below:

"I am now loving and approving of myself."

"I am always warm and loving toward self."

"I am easily able to maintain positive feelings about myself in any situation."

This will reinforce that importance of self-love. We are there for others more fully when we are also there for ourselves. In addition, we become role models, an inspiration to others, sparking them to love and honor themselves.

We need to generate this same body feeling with our self-love. A healthy love is gentle and compassionate and at the same time firm. We need to be kind and gentle with ourselves and at the same time institute a gentle firmness which leads us on our way.

Readers may also utilize daily self-hypnosis and repeat the following affirmations three times each prior to taking yourself into hypnosis:

1. "I am now loving and approving of myself."

2. "I am always feeling warm and loving toward myself."

3. "I am easily able to maintain positive feelings about myself in any situation."

Louise Hay, founder of Hay House Publishing, relays in her book: "Mirror Work," that 'mirror work' is extremely powerful in learning self-love and self-acceptance. She suggests looking into the mirror, looking deeply into your eyes, and repeating the following mantra: "I love myself unconditionally." Repeat this mantra for approximately one to two minutes. As the inner mind learns through repetition, this practice helps the mind replace past negative messages, replacing them with thoughts/feelings of self-love.

Add these to your daily affirmation process. Saying these words confidently while looking into your eyes as you do 'mirror work', will be very powerful. It may be uncomfortable initially, however, because the mind does learn through repetition, it will gradually feel more comfortable and natural.

Our ultimate goal is to accept ourselves unconditionally and expect the best from ourselves. We need to develop a warm embrace as we get in touch with our true feelings, thoughts and beliefs. Learning self-love helps us to resolve our painful experiences so that we can move on.

As we work together on self-love, my clients often share how they become aware of old, negative messages playing that kept them stuck in a life that isn't working as well as it should. I suggest that if they hear a replay of these old messages, don't resist since as noted previously, there is an old adage which wisely states that what we resist, persists. With that in mind, acknowledge their presence, thank them for sharing and then let them go. Doing this shifts the focus from the negativity, and toward loving ourselves for what we feel as we breathe into our feelings. By not judging self, but simply noticing thoughts and breathing as one would notice water flowing down a stream, we can begin to heal.

What often damages our self-esteem/self-love stems from our childhood experiences. Thus, it is so important to love and nurture the inner child as we saw in the previous chapter. For as we begin to love, accept and nurture the inner child, we make a permanent change in our self-love and self-esteem. As I have learned through my experience, subconscious memories and beliefs are difficult to influence with the 'logic' of the conscious mind.

However, in trance state, we can communicate directly and effectively with the subconscious and begin to challenge those long held negative beliefs. We can replace old negative programming, based on previous negative experiences with an accurate self-assessment based on an adult recognition of our strengths. We can literally erase old negative labels and learn forgiveness for mistakes. We can let go of old rules about what we should have been, how we should act, and what we should feel. Instead, we can tell our subconscious that we have always done our best, that we have legitimate needs, and we are worthwhile.

The basic task of hypnosis is to soften the judging parental voice (the inner critic.) Gradually, healing work done in trance state begins to have an effect. We begin to feel a growing sense of self-love and compassion for the person we are. The mind learns through repetition and as it took years of negative interactions to plant the negative voice in the subconscious, it just takes some time before the old programming lets go, being kind and gentle to ourselves in the process.

The mind is like a sponge, so during hypnosis it is absorbing every healing thought and positive suggestion. In the past, we have absorbed other's negative views and our own as well. As we access the subconscious mind, we can replace that negative programming with positive messages, beginning to see ourselves in a new light and reprogramming our subconscious with a positive self-image. Doing so can slowly begin to eliminate any old negative thoughts from the subconscious mind. We can release and erase all old negative self-images that no longer benefit us, beginning to develop a positive self-image, a new confidence and a deep and lasting self-love.

As this healing process continues, we can begin to enjoy using our subconscious mind to our advantage. Knowing that our subconscious always responds to our positive, loving suggestions. A new self-awareness and self-love begins to develop deep inside ourselves. We become aware that we are in control of our self-image and this causes us to have confidence in our growing self-love.

As we allow our own special qualities to grow and to surface, we recognize that each of us is unique and very special. Through this healing process, doubts are erased within the self and a true belief that we are more positive, confident and loving toward self emerges. We then easily are able to maintain positive feelings about ourselves in any situation.

Through the healing of the inner mind, a new self-love grows stronger each day. We can allow negative labels of the past to fade away, becoming balanced in mind, body and emotion. As the negativity is released and cleared, we begin to understand there are no mistakes in life, only lessons. Growth is a process of trial-and-error and experimentation. The so called 'failed' experiments are as much a part of the process as the experiment that ultimately 'works.' What we make of our lives is up to us and we have all the tools and resources within that we need.

It is a beautiful thing to hear my clients say that they

can now accept compliments from others easily and with pleasure. They realize they are good enough; they always have been and are learning to trust in themselves. A healthy balance begins to emerge as they enjoy taking time just for themselves, perhaps to soak in a bubble bath, or spend a quiet half hour reading or listening to favorite music. Whatever they enjoy the most.

Through the process of loving self, we can release any regrets from the past and grow and live for the future. A future filled with self-love and self-confidence.

In recent years, I have seen an increase in the number of clients who are caring for elderly parents. Though they have great love for their parents, they are also burned out and physically exhausted. Many times they are juggling full time work, marriage and children with caring for an elderly parent. Through the healing process of discovering the true self, releasing anger and healing the inner child, they begin to move into self-love and acceptance. As this occurs, they realize they must make changes in their lives. They must honor, love and value self just as they provide love and care for their parents and others. They become aware of the spirit of power within that enables them to overcome obstacles and improve the direction of their lives.

As I spoke to one such client caring for her elderly father, I could see Chloe's great resistance to suggestions for creating healthy boundaries. I explained how important it is for each of us to create healthy boundaries and to care for ourselves as we care for others. Chloe was emotionally, mentally and physically exhausted, yet, she refused to ask her siblings for help. Additionally, she was unable to say no to things she just couldn't do or did not want to do.

Due to this block to nurturing self-love, we did a regression to a significant memory in the past when she did not care for self. Chloe connected to a memory as an adolescent when her mother said it was selfish and wrong to say no to others. Her mind went quickly forward to other moments when her mother would repeat this same statement. As Chloe was guided to step into that younger body, she became aware of how this affected her on all levels in mind, body and spirit.

I asked her what resources she needed to change the outcome of these events, suggesting to bring in any help she may need from her adult self, her higher self , a loving relative, the choice was up to her. Chloe moved higher into spirit consciousness and brought in her higher self. This wise part of self helped her to move back to the beginning of these events and create a new, positive experience and a happy ending.

We allowed time for her to drift deeper and deeper into the new scene with its positive happy ending in order to be absorbed completely, becoming a permanent part of her reality and personality. It is very powerful to then move into a future scene with this healing in place. Thus, Chloe moved to a future scene where she had learned to take care of self, to a scene in which she had healed. She noticed how easily she could now take care of her emotional and physical needs.

As Chloe watched this scene unfold, she saw herself asking her siblings for help. They worked out a schedule, one that was fair to each of them. She felt the great love she had for her father and also felt great love for self simultaneously. I asked her to locate the place in her body where she felt these new, positive feelings. As Chloe breathed into this positive image, suggestions were given to breathe that new information into every cell, every thought and every emotion.

When Chloe emerged from hypnosis, she shared with me the beautiful and profound message she received from higher self. Gratefully, she allowed me to share this incredible message about loving and honoring self: " You do not need to measure up to anyone else's expectations of you. You are not on this earth for the purpose of being what someone expects you to be. You are you, you are unique, and you are fulfilling God's plan and purpose in your own special way. You do not owe it to any other person to be what he or she thinks you should be, your main purpose is to love and value self and to be and do what you came here to do. As you grow in honoring and loving self, your self-confidence continues growing stronger. You have within you the qualifications to handle any situation or circumstance that comes up in your life. You are developing the habit of performing actions that lead to health and happiness, knowing that once you establish that habit, it continues to work automatically. You will meet every challenge in your life with confidence, sureness and empowerment. Your faith and courage are becoming stronger and you keep developing a greater attitude of love and understanding for self and for others. Always remember that you grow stronger by learning from situations that are difficult. That will keep increasing your confidence and will enable you to handle any situation that comes up in your life. You know how to keep improving yourself and you know you are worthy of health and happiness. From now on you will anticipate happiness and joy and will expect good experiences. You are you, and you are very good."

With great emotion, Chloe told me she felt an inner renewal taking place. She could feel the healing flowing through her body, washing away the negative images from the past.

A lovely young woman in her thirties came to see me for deep seated feelings of worthlessness. As Vanessa spoke with me, it was clear these feelings had been with her for a very long time. She relayed that her mother had always been extremely critical. Her younger brother was favored quite openly, she described many such experiences in detail. Vanessa did very well academically yet her mother very seldom acknowledged this. She had a recording from her mother running in her unconscious mind, labeling her selfish and difficult. This was repeated quite often and so this manifested in feelings of worthlessness, deficiency and feeling damaged.

Many sessions centered around healing the inner child and bringing forth feelings of self-love, self-worth, self-trust and self-belief. As we have seen in the previous chapter, healing the inner child leads to these feelings of loving and honoring self.

What began to dawn on Vanessa was the realization that these negative labels never belonged to her. They belonged to the person who placed them upon her. As we worked together, Vanessa eventually forgave her mother and herself for believing these untrue statements that she was selfish and difficult. She also realized that her mother had a very difficult childhood and the above labels were the same her maternal grandmother had placed upon her mother.

To reinforce our work, I suggested a daily practice of placing her hands over her heart and sending love and compassion to the part of self that felt betrayed by her mother. Also, her own self for believing and identifying with these critical statements. As Vanessa did this daily practice, suggestions were also given to reassure that part that she will never abandon herself again. She will always be there with great love, compassion and care.

As Vanessa performed these healing activities, she described her heart opening and expanding. Allowing herself to love all the parts that she had previously rejected. In doing so, we create wholeheartedness, loving, supporting, accepting, and appreciating all parts of self. As we do this, we can then love others more fully, accepting those parts of others that are perhaps difficult to love. Thus, by loving self we become more loving to others. Our hearts expand and we are able to move into a place of nonjudgment of self and others. At the same time, being able to speak our truth in a loving, compassionate way.

Also, as Vanessa cleared away all the negative, critical labels and replaced them with feelings of self-love and self-worth, she automatically moved into alignment with higher self, her true self. This is a natural process as we clear away the layers that have prevented us from seeing our own true beauty and worth.

As Vanessa moved through this process of alignment with true self, she had a profound realization. She said she could see clearly that loving self is our true nature, yet it was covered over by a protected layer of fear. That is, fear to see the parts of self we do not like, do not want to be acknowledged, and do not want to accept. Vanessa's fear showed her how her mother and her own self had actually betrayed her. She feared trusting anyone to not hurt her, including trusting her own self.

Furthermore, she described how previously she wielded a tiny flashlight, casting a small beam of light, desperately trying to see her way through life. Now with this strong connection to true self, she shines a huge beam all around her. Vanessa can see her way through life, relationships, and circumstances with much greater clarity and wisdom.

In addition, Vanessa said she now completely understood when I described the need to see from the perspective of her 'vaster self.' This perspective allowed her to see her life with many more options and possibilities, permitting her to also realize the great importance of being there for others but most importantly being there for herself. Also, she now understands the importance of detaching from the family drama while simultaneously listening with loving care. Vanessa also obtained the ability to now say no in a loving way to things that were not in her best interests without guilt nor fear.

Higher self's wisdom shined upon all situations in her life, no longer allowing her to be involved with things that were not paramount to her peace of mind or heart. Loving self leads us all to greater connection to guidance from our true self aligning with our true path, purpose and passion.

It was extremely heartwarming to see this lovely soul blossom and radiate such a sense of self-worth, self-trust and self-belief. Slowly, Vanessa's relationship with her mother improved. This client's transformation was so noticeable that several members of her family came to see me for help. I felt very honored to be there not only for my client but also to help with the healing of her family.

I understand not only professionally but also personally the great importance of learning to love and honor self. I am honored to share a bit more of my story of how I recognized and aligned with my true self within and how I reached my true self utilizing this healing process. As I had mentioned in the beginning chapter, many years ago I utilized hypnosis practices and the practices I have described here, in order to overcome anxiety and stress. Hypnosis, techniques, visualizations and affirmations helped me to move forward from the anxiety and stress of my previous nursing positions. They also helped me to deal with issues from my childhood.

Learning and experiencing these healing processes, helped me to finally let go of many blocks and stories I still told myself. These issues were keeping me stuck and also safe in old unhealthy patterns. I did not know at the time that many years later this healing modality would bring me through a very traumatic time in my life.

Approximately five years ago after a routine mammogram, the radiologist asked to see me. She showed me the images and pointed out an area she believed was cancerous. I was in a state of shock and could not believe what was occurring. She was very compassionate and told me to consult with a surgeon immediately.

Within a week, the surgeon had scheduled a biopsy of this affected area. One week after the biopsy the surgeon called relaying that I did have breast cancer. I felt as if the floor beneath me opened up and swallowed me whole.

Though kind, the surgeon spoke at great length of frightening statistics, data and worst-case scenarios. He relayed that he believed it was an early stage but would not know the prognosis, not know exactly what we were dealing with until the final pathology report came in after surgery.

I struggled to hear and absorb his words. The surgery was scheduled for two weeks from that time. I had never felt so frightened in my life. Though my wonderful husband, my two loving children, friends and family were very compassionate and supportive, I felt vulnerable and traumatized. It would be approximately one month from the date of the mammogram before I knew my prognosis.

During that time, my head swam with all the horrible scenarios and data relayed by the surgeon. I somehow had to find a way to fulfill my roles as a wife, mother, daughter, sister, friend and therapist. During this time, I had also been caring for my elderly mother who had experienced a series of minor strokes two years prior. To say I was overwhelmed is an understatement!

As we have learned, we heal on all three levels: conscious mind, unconscious mind and on the level of spirit consciousness. Thus, I began the healing process from the level of conscious mind. The first technique to come to mind was to breathe deeply and slowly throughout the day. I also repeated affirmations to myself; to keep focused on positive thoughts so my mind would not run rampant with fear. For example, I would repeat:

"I am the power of healing and I am healing myself now."

"I am calm and strong."

In addition, I used a focus technique in order to stay

centered, present and grounded. I actually used this technique during the breast biopsy at the hospital. The procedure was very uncomfortable and went on at length because the surgeon was having difficulty finding the affected area. Though I was utilizing the slow, calm breathing, I knew I had to focus on something to bring me through.

Since I was instructed not to move during this procedure, my eyes searched the room for something to focus upon. I saw an image of a flower on the wall to my left. I focused on the color and imagined its aroma, texture, and where it may exist in nature. I continued to breathe calmly and slowly as I did this focusing technique. After the biopsy, the nurse asked me how I remained so calm and still during the uncomfortable, lengthy procedure. I described the above and she asked if she could share it with other patients. I felt so happy to know that this could help other women through this time.

I was initially healing on the conscious level, yet I understood the great importance of reaching the unconscious level as well. I knew I had to go deeply within in order to bring me through this time. As I awaited the surgery, I had great difficulty in sleeping. I would literally awaken every hour with the surgeon's voice in my head speaking of the frightening statistics and worst-case scenarios. So, in order to reach the unconscious mind, I loaded my MP3 player with various hypnosis meditations. I began to listen to these meditations as I fell asleep each night.

Initially I awakened frequently, with many fearful thoughts and feelings. However, I would replay the mediations throughout each and every night. Eventually, because the mind does learn through repetition, my mind became calmer as it received these positive healing suggestions on a very deep level. I also brought in prayer as I drifted deeply, asking for guidance, healing and feeling that Divine Support.

In addition, I practiced my daily self-hypnosis. As we have learned, it is a centering and grounding technique. It also increases the production of the neurotransmitter serotonin which promotes good sleep, improved mood, concentration and memory. I brought in the affirmations I had described earlier which I was using on a conscious level. I brought them in at this deeper, unconscious level of healing.

I repeated the following affirmations each day during self-hypnosis:

1. "I am calm, strong and balanced."
2. "I am the power of healing and I am healing myself now."
3. "I am happy and peaceful."

The suggestions given in hypnosis began to take root in my unconscious mind, replacing the past negative, frightening messages. I began to take back a sense of control over my life. As a nurse, I understood that the unconscious mind controls many, many bodily processes. Thus, it has great wisdom and an innate capacity to heal itself. Also, as the sacred writings tell us, "You can be transformed by the renewing of your mind." So as I renewed my mind with positive life, affirming thoughts, I aligned those thoughts and feelings with heart, in order to feel and become balanced in mind, body and spirit.

One week after surgery, the final pathology report revealed the malignancy was stage O. Surgery had removed the entire affected area and there would be no need for any further surgery. Feelings of great relief and gratitude for answered prayers swept through me. I was then scheduled for one month of daily radiation which would lessen the chance that the cancer would recur.

During daily radiation, I utilized the calm, deep breathing as well as visualization. I visualized the beam of radiation as white light that would not harm me in any way. It would only prevent the cancer from recurring. I also continued listening to guiding mediations each night before falling asleep. My sleep had improved greatly at this point. Also, I continued my daily practice of self-hypnosis, reinforcing the healthy, positive suggestions. The visualizations, affirmations, self-hypnosis, and the techniques I have shared throughout this book, helped me tremendously.

Utilizing these tools helps us to take back control of our lives during difficult times. We learn how to relax the mind and body whenever we begin to feel fear and anxiety.

As we continue to access the unconscious mind, we begin to understand on this deep level that any illness or storm in our life is a valuable gift which forces us to slow down and look at our life. As I continued to go within, I asked my true self for guidance as to why this had occurred. For no matter how unpleasant something is, it is always teaching us something. There is a growth lesson, we need only go within and trust what we find. During my daily self-hypnosis, I could see that though I had gratefully healed many layers in the past, there was more which needed to heal.

As I continued to connect on the level of spirit consciousness, I gained greater clarity around that which remained to be healed. I realized that I had taken on way too much. Though I loved my work, I was putting in too many hours in my practice each week. I also support my clients with emails in between sessions which I am honored to do. The first change I put into place was to cut back on the amount of time at work. It was very difficult because I love helping others, but I knew that this illness was a wake-up call. I slowly put changes in place to cut back on my hours. Also, I started a waiting list for those new clients who wished to see me. I was very pleasantly surprised to discover that prospective clients were amendable to being placed on a waiting list.

Spirit consciousness helped me to see that I also needed help with my dear mother. I was guided to contact an organization and within twenty-four hours I found a beloved soul who would come twice a week to help with my mother. I felt a weight lifting as this changed took place. She was a true angel and my mom adored her.

During this time, as I continued to connect to the level of spirit, I knew I had to speak my truth, of course in a very, loving kind way. Though I had learned to put up boundaries previously through my healing work, I didn't realize there remained a few people in my life who I found it very difficult to say no to. Healing from this trauma on the conscious level and unconscious level took me to this level of spirit consciousness.

It became very clear that I had to learn to say no to those few remaining individuals in my life. I started to say no to others when I knew it would drain and overwhelm me. I never wanted to experience cancer or have my husband or children go through that agony again. This realization strengthened my commitment to put up even stronger boundaries with love and compassion.

Though I still do not enjoy saying no, even when needed, through practice, it has become easier. Also, please remember that healing is a process. There were times and continue to be times that I slip into old unhealthy behavior. However, I catch it more and more quickly and give great love and compassion to that part of self.

Through my experience, I believe the most important piece is to make that commitment to self, to loving self. To ask for Divine support for the strength to stay focused and committed to healing goals. As we trust in that Divine support and as we connect more and more fully to our true self, we begin knowing that we are never alone and can always draw on that support especially in the midst of challenging days.

I could see that the illness was a great gift. It forced me to put up those remaining boundaries, speak up for myself, and know the great importance of loving myself. Illness forced me to know I deserved and needed to have a life that was much more in balance. I started doing my artwork again which I had not done for many, many years. Also, I began taking hour long hikes in the woods with a dear friend, an activity which I loved but never had the time to do.

At times clients will ask me, "what does it look like to love yourself?" "How do you do that?" So, I share with them what was described here, that is, utilizing hypnosis and the various tools/techniques which have been discussed. In doing so, we clear the layers that prevented us from completely honoring and loving ourselves. Especially layers around guilt for saying no in order to give ourselves loving care.

I also share that for me, loving self involves checking in with myself, assuring myself that I will no longer allow myself to be drained and overwhelmed. For me, taking a pause, taking a breath before I say 'yes' helps me to be sure it is something I feel guided to do not something I feel obligated to do. If I feel guided to say 'no', depending on the situation, I will offer options/suggestions to that individual, allowing them to find their own way which allow them to grow and trust in self.

As I mentioned, I do not enjoy saying no but I still understand at a deep level the need to do so. Also, I find time each day to do self-hypnosis, physical exercise and eating healthy food. It is definitely challenging some days but I find my way clear to put this into daily practice as best I can. Not doing it perfectly, but just remaining committed to this important practice.

In addition, it is knowing that we are always connected to the Divine and are worthy of that love, support, connection and guidance. Also, for me loving self is tapping into my passions. What do I love to do? What fills me up? When I consider these things, I can continue to give to others in balance.

Finally, in my life, loving self means being there for myself, to never again abandon myself in over caretaking or in any other way, to not betray myself, to have my own back so to speak.

As I was healing through post-surgery and radiation, I

used the technique of placing my hands over my heart each and every day. I dropped out of all the myriad thoughts of the mind and into the feeling of my heart. I sent great compassion and love to all the parts that were so frightened and wounded. As this continued, my heart expanded and I could feel love filling me up and spilling out to others.

Please ponder this question readers. "What does it mean for you to love and honor yourself?" As you do your daily self-hypnosis and utilize the various tools and techniques which resonate with you, these new positive thought patterns will align heart and mind. You will know what changes you wish to put into place in order to love and honor self. It is a process, it is a dance, one step forward two steps back but you are moving gradually forward. Please give yourself much credit for even the smallest of changes because this means that the seeds have been planted, so they will continue to grow and flourish.

Connecting even more strongly to my true self opened me up to receiving greater clarity and messages during my self-hypnosis and in my dreaming state. It also deepened my faith and trust in the Divine. My healing work with clients has deepened and my heart comes from this deeper level of compassion, empathy and understanding. I can see how the storms and challenges in our lives equal transformation. Whatever storm we may be experiencing, whether it is health, relationship, finance, business, whatever we are experiencing, we need only go within.

We understand the great importance of loving self, of giving great compassion and loving care to the parts of self that are in pain. The parts that most need this tender care

are traumatized, wounded and afraid. Through utilizing the tools and techniques we heal on the conscious, unconscious and on the level of spirit consciousness. As we do this, we learn the great truth that to love self, to honor self is the greatest gift we can bestow upon ourselves. For we bring balance, peace, and joy into our lives.

This spills out from us to others, thus loving ourselves helps us love others even more. We have more to give, we are not drained any longer, resentful and frustrated. We see ourselves as worthy and deserving of a life connected to our passions and how we can express this in our daily life. This is a process and as we honor this process, we honor ourselves. We renew our minds with thoughts and ideas based on self-love, self-worth, self-trust, and self-belief. Learning to love ourselves brings greater joy in our lives. Through this process, we connect to our Divinity and begin to see ourselves through the eyes of the true self, no longer allowing what has been to hold us back or down any longer.

As we move into loving and honoring self, we continue to support others as we accept support. We achieve a balance between the two and find the difference between what we think we 'should' do and what our heart really desires. Through this process, we begin to alter our behavior in a very healthy way in order to achieve this balance all while considering what we could do to support others while still feeling good about ourselves. Imagine how good and healthy it would feel to state how we are feeling emotionally and then suggest a compromise. Our goal is to remain supportive while taking care of our own needs.

As we establish our limits and boundaries within each

situation, we take full charge of what is our duty and let go of that which is not. In doing so, we find more enjoyment supporting others as we create more harmonious relationships. Most importantly, healthy boundaries create a more harmonious and loving relationship with self and reduce stress and anxiety in our lives.

The following visualization is a journey within to generate self-love:

Please take five slow deep breaths... settle more and more deeply into your safe sanctuary... allow yourself to expand with each breath... please stay open to the guidance and loving support that exists on this journey... allow your intuition to 'hear' and 'see' these messages... Right now there may be things about yourself that you do not see as being loveable... by releasing your hold on the qualities you do not like, you will begin to recognize you are powerful beyond measure.

I would like for you to become willing to let go and see yourself through new eyes... In your mind's eye, see yourself as you think you are... examine yourself from all sides... allow the things you dislike about yourself to come to mind and then, just as quickly, let them go... continue to see yourself from all angles... Now, imagine yourself in a serene forest... There are a gentle deer living in this forest... think about the deer's gentle, compassionate spirit... the deer embodies the gentleness of spirit that heals all wounds... by finding qualities to love about yourself, your lack of self-love will melt away... deer asks that you apply gentleness to learning self-love... as you rest quietly... in this safe place... imagine you become a deer.

Now, from deer's space, examine yourself again... What does deer notice about you?... What qualities does deer admire in you?... feel deer's gentle, loving support... What message does deer have for you right now?... Think about the parts of yourself that you dis-

like... it's time now to let that go... think about how the rain washes the earth, leaving it clean, fresh and new... as you stand in that magical forest... imagine that you are standing in a warm, gentle rain... that clear, pure rain washes away everything about yourself that you now find disagreeable.

Rest quietly and allow the rain to work its magic... you are now ready to fill yourself back up... let's invite other loving beings into this magical, nurturing space... is there someone in your life who has loved you unconditionally?... if so, think about that person and invite them to join you... you may invite in your guardian angel... and your true self... stand in a circle with this loving group and hold hands... ask each to share with you what they love most about you... take your time... feel all the love this group has for you... open your heart and let it fill you... from this moment forward, see yourself through the eyes of this loving supportive group... all the love and compassion that you've given to others is now also directed inward... the more loving and compassionate you are toward yourself, the more love and compassion you have to share with others... filled to the core with self-love... Claim it... it is your birthright and you deserve it... slowly opening your eyes filled with self-love.

May this meditation take you even deeper into experiencing self-love and self-acceptance:

Please close your eyes and begin breathing deeply and slow five times. You can set your timer or simply allow yourself to open your eyes, fully alert and awake at the end of this meditation as you count slowly from one to five.

Now imagine yourself in a peaceful place... anyplace you wish... it could be a beach with a nice breeze blowing or a mountain area with a lake and clean fresh air... or a peaceful place in your imagination... all things are possible in this private, safe, peaceful place... as you drift deeper and deeper... as your mind opens more to aware-

ness and understanding... you realize you were made by the same Creator Source Who created each of us... as your mind aligns with this truth... you are aware of that Divine spark within... the true Divinity of who you are... one with the Creator Source... a co-creator of your reality... you realize the truth of the following spiritual statement; "You can be transformed by the renewing of your mind."

As you renew your mind now with positive, uplifting thoughts... you transform your life and begin now to accept your true worth... your true self... acceptance of who you are... connecting to this true self... who like an internal coach, guides you from within... its function is the past and the present... you then understand there is no need to be whatever those past negative memories represent... your true inner self understands that you can be completely liberated from the past... you feel an inner transformation taking place... as you grow stronger by learning from situations that are difficult... you break free from the past and create a present and future full of love, prosperity, health, happiness, peace and joy.

Now seeing self standing at the top of a grand staircase... you begin to slowly descend the staircase as you slowly count backwards from ten to one... each number takes you deeper down... the steps are safe with a thick, soft carpeting... a very gentle decline... handrail firm... on the last number you step off that last step... and find yourself in a magical place... A place where all things are possible... and so now , counting slowly backwards from ten to one... ten... stepping down safely and gently... nine... eight drifting down... seven... six... five... half way there now... four... further and further down... three... two... one... stepping safely off that bottom step now... the ground soft beneath your step... you see a small cottage... it is painted in your favorite color... you walk across the stone walkway leading to the cottage... you have reached the front door... it is *ajar, as if this magical place was waiting just for you.*

You walk in and close the door behind you... you notice the beautiful furnishings... the carpeting... the lovely pictures on the walls... you notice a cozy, inviting recliner... you walk over and recline in it... so safe... so cozy... comforting... soft, relaxing music fills the air... the following thoughts come to you... they fill you and transform you with their loving energy... I wish to rest and repair... I am calm and secure... I am peaceful... I am free... cleared of any preconceived thoughts... I now love myself unconditionally as I release the past... I am safe and loved... I am loved... I am that I am that I am... a being truly reborn... transformed by the renewing of my mind.

The unconscious mind realizes you are the creator of the slate... you are now a new slate... the slate of life... you are the writer that would put on the slate what positive loving, healthy things you desire... if you want to create something... you bring in the feeling energy of the joy from the heart center... you have freed yourself from the demands and expectations from yourself and others... you are now a new slate... imbued with this new energy... no longer allowing what has been, had held you back... down... or from believing in self... this new energy imbued in you and through you... as the writer you bring in what you want for your life... for yourself... a co-creator with the Divine.

Perhaps you are writing, I wish to be in joy... and to be in joy is to at Peace... and to be at Peace is to remember that you are loved beyond measure... loved as the divine beautiful Light that you are... and there is nothing that you have to do to earn it... as this is your birthright... take your time and write on your slate what positive, healthy things you wish to bring into your life... Now you begin to rise from the recliner in the cottage... and move back toward the door from which you entered... you open the door and slowly head down the path... away from the cottage... you see the staircase which led you to this magical place... and now, slowly begin to ascend the stairs and on the count of ten you are back and reoriented to your surroundings... you bring back with you all the healing which has taken place today... so beginning to count now... one... two... on the count of ten you will be back to full awareness, fully alert and refreshed... three... four... five... six... seven... eight... nine... on the next number you are back in a wide awake, fully alert state feeling very, very good... and ten... back in a wide awake fully alert state feeling balanced in mind, body and spirit.

CHAPTER SIX

"Living With Inner Peace"

"I am peaceful, and I am safe."
"Peace abides within me at all times."
"I choose to be peaceful and calm throughout my daily life."

As we move through the previous healing steps of aligning with the truth within, creating a healing space, releasing layers of anger and resentment, then moving into the heart space and healing and nurturing the inner child which allows us to love and honor self, we then create a life filled with inner peace. We recognize the truth that peace lays within our very core, abiding throughout the ups and downs of everyday life.

When we are at this stage of the healing process, one of the benefits noticed by clients is that the chatter of the conscious mind becomes much quieter. Since the mind and body are connected, when the mind relaxes, the body relaxes. This reminds us that whatever the external circumstances, peace and harmony belong to us.

We begin to open up to the best that the world has to offer us. As we bring peace and harmony into our lives, we become aware it is possible to make changes in our life in a comfortable, easy way. This leads us to the willingness to make changes in our lives, knowing we are safe and secure. We are also aware of the capability of meeting all challenges with calmness, flexibility and confidence.

It is a joy to see clients lives coming into balance as they learn to experience life as more tranquil. An ability to choose to experience life in the most positive way comes forth strongly, making the decision that internal peace and harmony are our new reality, now and in the future. For it is our right to have a calm mind, and to be internally calm and peaceful.

To reach this stage, the previous work on releasing anger and resentment must be integrated. As a result, clients are able to release any people and situations from the past that had been unhelpful to them, through forgiveness. They are able to take back their power and decide which persons, situations and experiences will no longer have a hold over them.

They are able to put past situations into perspective, knowing that when we put past situations in perspective, we release their hold over us. When we let go of negative experiences of the past, we release their hold over us. When we forgive others who have wronged us, we release their hold over us.

As they are able to do this, they become aware of their freedom. Also, that great courage and power exist within them. Thus, they are able to move on to the next moment, and the next in a positive and peaceful way.

During this healing process, clients become aware of the capability of leaving judgment to the Creator. Realizing that as they release this need to judge, they are able to appreciate and love themselves just as they are. This leads to the ability to accept others around them just as they are, being able to forgive, and to love and to appreciate themselves as they are.

They choose to see humor in life as well as harmony and joy in the midst of everyday life. Through this healing process, they become aware of the opportunity that has arisen to practice accepting self as well as the opportunity to practice accepting others. This brings forth the opportunity to also believe in themselves in each and every moment and to choose thoughts and words that will nourish and support themselves and others.

During this healing process, clients become more and more open to new awareness. They become more receptive to their intuitions and are able to trust their own decisions, becoming filled with loving and positive thought patterns. As they continue to move more deeply into this healing, their spirit becomes lovingly cultivated.

A client who had done incredible work releasing anger, healing the inner child and reclaiming her self-love and self-worth was having difficulty trusting moments of peace. Sara was so grateful to have moved into this stage of healing and her past issues with anxiety and stress in her daily life, were now a thing of the past. Though there were stressful times, she now reacted with healthy, positive responses. If there were moments when she felt any old healthy reactions, she fearlessly stayed with those feelings and loved herself through it.

Sara continually asked her higher self for guidance and forged a deeper and deeper connection to her true self. In addition, she practiced self-hypnosis each day and utilized the various techniques /tools I have described here. Yet, as her daily life thus became more peaceful, she described a part of herself which did not trust it would last. These feelings/thoughts were described as 'waiting for the other shoe to drop.' We did work around accessing this part of self that did not feel safe nor trusting with these feelings of peace.

As Sara drifted deeply into trance, I asked her to imagine stepping into her private sanctuary. I had her enjoy all those feelings. Then, I addressed that part of self that felt uncomfortable being at peace. I asked that part to please step forward and make itself known or seen in whatever way felt most safe and comfortable. I then let that part know it had done a very good job of creating this fear of peace for its own reasons. I also relayed that I knew its reasons are really, in its mind at least, for Sara's highest good. But I also let that part know that this fear of peace was not appreciated nor welcomed at all by the main part of Sara.

So I addressed the client and asked that the part of her that feels fearful about peace, I am going to ask it to transform. I addressed that part and asked it to use its power and strength to manifest something that is more life affirming for Sara such as comfort and relaxation being at peace and trusting in that peace. That part relayed to me it was creating the fear of peace in order to keep Sara safe. This beloved soul had experienced much trauma in her life and though she had moved through the healing stages beautifully, there was this part that was still unsure if it could really trust, or feel safe being peaceful.

I explained that Sara was no longer willing to experience this fear of peace any longer. I thanked that part for doing such a great job and looking out for her. Further dialogue with that part involved thanking it for helping her through very difficult times in her life. Now that her healing had taken place, it was actually holding her back, but we needed that part because it was so powerful and an important part of her. I then asked if it was willing to change jobs so that from now on Sara could feel safe and comfortable being at peace. As the unconscious mind contemplated this, I then suggested that this part of self is very good at what it does. So I asked that part, as well as Sara herself to listen at the deepest levels.

It was then suggested that Sara knew how to frighten herself, how to not trust in peace, being able to hold onto peaceful thoughts and feelings. For if you think something is upsetting then it causes you to feel upset , unsure of the capacity and ability to be peaceful .But I am also sure that you also know that there are other things you can think of that are comforting and calming.

These are thoughts and images that are relaxing and re-assuring and can help you to feel safe; trust you are safe to be peaceful. You can let your deeper inner mind distract you with calm, peaceful and pleasant thoughts and feelings and I believe that after a while, you will be unable to even remember how to worry in the ways you have done before. So from now on whenever you come upon that situation in that the past has caused you to know trust nor feel safe being at peace, you can enter it knowing you are protected. You can know that you are cared for by your higher self and can always trust in that guidance. And you can let that fearful part of you know that you aren't interested in being afraid of peace anymore.

You can thank that part for trying to protect you, but you are not in danger any longer. You have healed from those traumatic experiences of the past. And so that part can rest until its really needed to keep you safe. For now, that fearful part, the part that does not feel safe or trusting to be at peace, can take a back seat and let calmness and peacefulness come forward in your life. They can remind you instead of the good things than can happen in your life, of the calmness that is your right, of the peace that belongs to you. Because those old thoughts and fears are no longer helpful to you.

So I talked further to that part and suggested that it rest until there is a time, and there may never be a time, that it may need to warn Sara. However, if such a time arises, it could then use its voice. Further suggestions were given to that fearful part to allow calmness and peace to flow into Sara. Also, that the old thoughts and fears around being at peace were being released because they are no longer useful. All parts of self are choosing peace and calmness.

So you can relax, and go about your life and you might be very surprised to discover you have been thinking of something else entirely. And when that happens, you'll know at that point, deep down in every cell of your body, and every part of you, both seen and unseen, that you'll never need to experience that old fear of peace again. That it's over and done with, more quickly than you ever expected. So you can relax now and be filled with different thoughts and different feelings. Those of peace, safe to be at peace, trusting in peace, calmness and safety. And as all this peace and calmness and safety flows in, you begin to feel very secure and very happy. And notice how easily you now simply choose the life experience that you prefer.

Further work was done with the unconscious mind and the higher self to signal to us that part had indeed changed jobs. We then anchored the feelings of peace, safe and trusting to be at peace as she touched together her right index finger to thumb. That is, taking a deep breath in, thinking the word 'peace' as she touched her right index finger to thumb, then exhaling slowly and letting go of those fingers.

You may feel guided to utilize this technique whenever you need to fill yourself with peaceful energy. Each time you use this technique or any that have been described in the chapters, you are regaining a sense of control over your life. When we feel more in control we actually can let go at a deeper level. When we don't feel in control, we feel we cannot let go because we will lose it. However, as you discover that sense of healing in your life, you realize you can let go. You can get a sense of control back anytime you want it or need it. No one around you will be the wiser, as you practice this technique or any, about the power you have in your life. You can then wonder about what other things you are going to experience and practice and learn. Suggestions were then given to make that simple connection whenever Sara wanted to feel that safety and trustfulness to be at peace and to allow herself to feel peaceful without fear.

At our next session, Sara relayed feeling so joyful about allowing herself to finally experience peace in her life, free of any fear that it is not safe to do so. She utilized her anchor of touching her right index finger to thumb throughout the day, in order to reinforce the healing work she had done. Trusting in her higher self to guide her and that part to now work with her, helping her to feel safe and trusting to be at peace.

Very interestingly, I experienced something similar during my healing process. As I worked through issues around anxiety, stress, and the trauma of the breast cancer diagnosis, I was more and more connected to my higher self. I felt a deep transformation of past fears and moved into a sense of self-love and a connection to my true self, path, passion and purpose. Yet, as the inner journeying brought me to a sense of peace, I doubted that I could hold onto that peace.

I continued to do my daily self-hypnosis; speaking with my higher self who I knew had the answer. Also, I prayed for Divine support daily. Various messages came through as I did this healing practice. The first message I recall was seeing myself in the mammography facility. I saw this part of myself still stuck there, so to speak. I could sense that a part of myself had not completely processed all that happened. I dialogued with her asking higher self to help. The words which came through were about how she would never feel safe again. That the 'rug would be pulled out from under her' again and she would never be able to fully be at peace. I visualized holding that part's hand and standing under a beautiful cleansing waterfall, as I described earlier in one of our visualizations. I saw and felt heavy weights leaving the mind and body as I completed the visualization.

During another self-hypnosis practice, I saw a vision of my mother. During the five years I was very honored to help my mother after the series of strokes, I realized, through this vision, how it affected my lack of trust to be in peace. Multiple times throughout the day I would check on her and bring her meals, snacks and so on. I also needed to take her on all appointments as well as errands and church services each weekend.

She was on an anti-coagulant to prevent future strokes. Each time, she would be fine for a while and then the medication would cause her to have internal bleeding. The cardiologist changed the medication each time this happened, however, after a time it would begin again. So, I would be checking on her in between clients and due to my nursing background, I would see signs that she was again bleeding internally. Each time we would have to go immediately to the emergency room so that she could receive transfusions and monitoring.

Other unexpected medical issues would pop up as well. My unconscious mind said that it could never really rest because there was always a possibility of an emergency situation. I called on higher self to help this part of my mind understand this situation was no longer occurring. That is, sadly a few years ago just after my mother's ninety-fourth birthday she stood up and her right leg gave way. She fell and fractured her right hip.

After surgery, she had to be transferred to a rehab facility. Though she had ongoing therapy, she did not recover use of her ability to walk. In addition, the surgeon believed she had suffered minor strokes while in surgery. Thus, her cognitive ability declined. Due to all the above changes, she sadly could not return home and requires ongoing care at the rehab facility where she now resides. Though it saddens me deeply, I explained how we are no longer solely responsible for her.

We visit often and are involved in monitoring her care. I do feel it is essential to have an integral role her care, including frequent visits, calls and meetings with the care staff. However, not at the previous level of being solely responsible. Since the part can now rest, I thanked it for doing its job, for being hypervigilant about my mother's care but now it could rest and allow peace to come forward. I could feel myself almost 'sigh' as the unconscious mind let go of the hypervigilance. When we can move an emotion, in this case not feeling safe to be at peace, to a vaster awareness, we are able to deal with it.

Through hypnotic technique we replace old limiting negative beliefs with new neural pathways (through repetition of our hypnosis practice /tools and techniques). Then release and reframe, thus bringing about new ways to think, believe, and react to old and new situations.

As I continued to 'check in' with these two parts of self and work with them, the healing continued. Each time I felt any trigger when I was peaceful, I placed my hands over my heart and spoke to those parts reassuring them that we were letting go of the grip the old negative energy held on us.

During this time another message came forth while in trance. I saw a board with some areas vividly lit and others darkened. My eyes scanned the board for all the places I saw lit up. I asked higher self what this meant. I received guidance that the areas I was seeing represented that which

I was to help others see. I actually heard "to help others see clearly." They were 'pieces of the puzzle' which represented my soul's purpose in helping others understand what was needed in order that they may heal. I understood the great importance of helping others to come to their true self and to be able to see from this vaster self's perspective.

Through my experience, all the darkness, and pain we unfortunately experience through various times of our life, take us to higher and higher levels. Yet, we need to find a way to see through the pain, to be able to process it and then let it go, allowing us to embrace fully who we truly are.

As I gradually was able to trust being at peace, I could see the great importance of sharing this with others and how vitally important it is to see ourselves as spiritual beings having a human existence, not the other way around. For by seeing ourselves as a spiritual being, we recognize that is the truth of who we really are. Yet we must heal from the pain, hurt, anger, bitterness, trauma, and grief the human part of self experiences. As we continue to move through this series of inner healing as described previously, we then access our higher self. This true self helps us to see why things are happening as they are. Why we are triggered, feeling anxious, stressed, fearful, worried, not enough, not worthy and so on. Each time we are triggered, is an opportunity to heal, to see what lies beneath the pain of that negative emotion.

Having the awareness of who we truly are, allows us to see things that are meant to be. As we tap into that awareness, especially during difficult and challenging times, we see how these circumstances allowed us to grow. If we only see from the eyes of ego so to speak, we see only pain and become mired in anger, resentment, hurt, anxiety, fear; refusing to see any lessons we are to learn. We refuse to see the part of self, which is crying out to be healed, calling out for our attention, our loving care and nurturing.

Through accessing higher self, we realize that which triggers us to heal, to accelerate our soul growth as very important growth lessons disguised as 'mistakes' or things that shouldn't be occurring. This helps us to accept the part of self that is wounded, developing great compassion, even pride for the part of self that we had previously rejected. That part endured a very difficult time. It took it on as a way to grow, evolve, and transform our lives in powerful ways.

In addition, we realize through this process we are in non-peace when we reject that part of ourselves that is wounded and/or reject a circumstance which occurs. By allowing our true self, our vaster self, to come forward, we see through 'metaphysical eyes' not physical eyes. In doing so, we open our eyes to see clearly. We begin to understand that in every event good and bad there are spiritual treasures unfolding. When we open our eyes via the true self, we will find them. Here lies an opportunity to find the richness behind the challenges and difficulty.

Within every soul there is a knowing, but we forget. We turn away, not wanting to see the suffering, not wanting to deal with it. But we know that within us is the true self who urges us to look, to behold and to see. That true self wants us to explore the knowing there is more to life and to existence than everyday human reality and explore the spiritual reality behind what is happening physically. It allows us to move into acceptance. Acceptance is the key to peace. We reach this acceptance through healing at all the stages we have learned about. Acceptance of true self will not only help to see the truth in each situation but also provides support and that connection to the Divine, knowing we are never alone.

As I was guided to write this book, I realized how much I had healed through this process. If I identified with the human/ego self, I felt very vulnerable in sharing my story and to be seen and heard for my work and beliefs. Yet, because I am now able to bring forth my true self, I can understand the importance of sharing all I have learned professionally and personally with others. I would also like to share the importance of setting the intention and commitment to heal.

Once again, it is a 'dance', we move forward and back as we progress. It is not about doing it perfectly. It is about loving, trusting, accepting and believing in our ability to heal. We must give great compassion and love to the parts of self that feel they have missed the mark and to honor that intention and commitment to move forward in our lives as we reach for healing, balance and peace. We do this all while knowing that we deserve it, that we are worthy of it and it is the nature of our true selves.

Part of this step in healing is also the realization of the importance to live in the present moment. In truth, time does not exist, what we refer to as the 'past' and 'future' has no reality. We have constructed this concept of time to suit our own needs. We have only this moment.

We keep regrets and upsets about the past alive in our

minds by constantly recalling old memories. We feel anxiety about the future by imagining negative scenes of what may happen. We release regrets and upsets from the past and alleviate concerns about the future, by bringing our attention to the present moment. This cultivates the practice of peace in our lives. Bringing forth the ability to come from this place of inner peace.

Please think about this question: Do you actually experience the passing of time or just the passing of thoughts?

During this phase in healing, regression work is done to recall a memory from the past that continues to affect the present. As I did this work with my client, Theresa, she became aware of a negative memory concerning a friend. She felt very betrayed and hurt by this friend. She realized how often she relived this memory. I asked her if there was a lesson for her to learn by constantly recalling this memory and if so, what could she do to learn this lesson and move on.

She relayed to me that by holding onto it, she felt as if she was protecting herself, wanting to be sure that it would never occur again in another relationship. I asked her unconscious mind to retain all wisdom, learning, and lessons from this experience but to let all the hurt, negativity and toxicity go. As she released the memory, her mind became clear and she was able to simply be in the present moment. She also relayed to me she learned that her discernment protected her. Through this past unpleasant experience with her friend, Theresa now had the discernment to choose relationships that would be safe for her and nourishing for her life. She immediately felt a relaxation in her mind and body; a peacefulness that washed over her.

We then had her imagine a concern for the future, something that often worries her. Theresa brought a future thought that was affecting her enjoyment of the present moment. I guided her to see in what way does this future image impact her present moment. Also, if there were any benefits to continuing worrying about this future event. Her unconscious mind brought forth her concern about her financial future. Theresa realized how much it negatively impacts her enjoyment of the present moment. The benefit of continuing to worry about this, had to do with her unconscious belief that she could control the future by obsessing over it. As she was guided to release this image, clear her mind and simply be in this moment, she allowed herself to rest in the present moment. Her unconscious mind then began to generate creative solutions to this worry. One of them involved consulting with a financial planner so that she could feel secure about her financial future.

Theresa then imagined the life she would create when she lived fully in the present moment, free of past regrets and worries about the future. As this session continued, I asked her to notice any thoughts about the past or future that may be passing through her mind right now and to let them go, to breathe into the moment. As the session continued, it was suggested that as thoughts come into her mind, to label them as either 'past' or 'future', then let them go and turn her attention to her breath. Just focusing on the air passing in and out of her nostrils. Then to ask herself, if she had any problems or upsets right then, in that instant, as she returned her focus to her breath.

As this stage of healing continues, clients realize that their power resides in the present moment, not in the past nor in the future. During this practice of being in the moment, they enhance their personal power. They also learn to quiet the negative 'chatterbox' within. During this learning process, they develop the ability to choose only positive thoughts and images, shifting out non-peaceful thoughts and images more and more quickly. As this occurs, it becomes easier and easier to connect with positive, peaceful thoughts and ideas.

The unconscious mind has learned to automatically shift away from the negative thoughts and connect to the positive thoughts and images. They are able to find and listen to that positive voice within in the midst of any situation. This voice is also known as the higher self and resides on the level of spirit consciousness. This part of self is filled with great wisdom and helpful, positive ideas. As we move into the realm of spirit consciousness, the client moves into that space of beauty and serenity.

The following is a wonderful technique to help move readers into this level of spirit consciousness and communicate with higher self. First, close your eyes and take five or six slow deep breaths. Imagine being a safe, sacred sanctuary; it could be a beautiful garden or a wooded glen, whatever you choose. Then invite your higher self to join you in that place. An image then begins to form of the oldest, kindest, wisest part of self. It has been described by clients in many ways----a wise old man or woman, as a friendly animal or bird, an angel, a ball of light, an old friend, a relative or religious figure.

Accept your higher self as it appears, wise, kind and compassionate. You will easily sense its caring for you and its wisdom. Invite your higher self to make itself comfortable there with you. And now, ask it to assist you in learning to be more positive/peaceful and release stress and anxiety.

Ask this advisor what steps you can take to release the negativity that has been holding you back from really enjoying life. Listen carefully to your advisor's response. You may imagine your advisor talking with you or you may simply have a direct sense of its message in some other way. Allow yourself to communicate in whatever way seems most natural.

Continue the conversation until you feel you have learned all you can at this time. Take a few minutes and consider what your advisor has told you. How would your life change if you released negativity and learned to be more positive and optimistic? As you imagine this, do you see any obstacles or problems using this advice? If so, how would you deal constructively with these obstacles? If you need more information here, please ask your advisor.

When your communication is finished, thank your higher self for helping you. Ask it to tell you the easiest and surest way to make contact. Realize that you can call another meeting with your advisor whenever you feel the need. Say goodbye for now in whatever way seems most appropriate.

Another powerful tool is to imagine a waterfall for cleansing. Begin by closing the eyes and taking five or six slow, deep breaths. Then visualize or imagine you are taking a walk on a beautiful path in the woods. Up ahead is a clearing and you can hear the water moving down stream. At the end of this stream is a beautiful pool and waterfall; you feel drawn to stand under the waterfall. It is just the right temperature and just the right flow. You feel there is magic in the pool, something quite beautiful and mysterious.

As the water flows over you and through you it releases anything that no longer serves you. All past hurts, resentments, bitterness, frustration, anger, guilt, rejection and negative thoughts and feelings are just being sent out of your body, cleansing and purifying your mind, body and spirit. It is transmuting and transfiguring all of these unhelpful energies, emotions and experiences.

The magical waterfall transmutes and transforms all these old negative energies which had once held you back; freeing you completely. It takes all that no longer serves you away, no matter how distant or recent. As all of these heavy, burdensome, unhelpful and unhealthy energies, experiences, thoughts, and so on are being lifted and released by the cleansing waterfall, you keep feeling lighter and lighter. The release fills you with peace, calmness, tranquility and serenity. You remain in this healing visualization for a few moments as you soak in all of this positive energy.

Self-hypnosis is also very beneficial in bringing about this sense of peace and calm. Thus, prior to taking yourself into hypnosis, please repeat each of the following affirmations three times:

"I am at peace and I am safe."

"Peace abides within me at all times."

"I choose to be peaceful and calm throughout my daily life."

As you repeat this self-hypnosis exercise, the inner mind becomes filled with different thoughts and different feelings; those of peace, calmness and serenity. You may also wish to add the above self-hypnotic suggestions to your daily affirmation practice:

"I am at peace and I am safe."

"Peace abides within me at all times."

"I choose to be peaceful and calm throughout my daily life."

Perhaps you can place your hands over your heart and feel the energy of peace transverse your body and mind as you say the above words.

The following visualization is healing and reinforces a sense of inner peace:

Please close your eyes and breathe deeply and slowly five times. Then imagine yourself in your sacred sanctuary. Your healing space… a place you feel safe, supported and comfortable.

Please use your imagination… imagine yourself standing at the top of a flight of steps… as you look down the stairs, you notice there are ten steps leading down to a beautiful lawn at the bottom… across the lawn is a pathway which leads you into a magical garden.

In a moment… begin counting from ten down to one… as you do, you will go down a step each time you think a number… as you slowly go down the steps and walk across the path to the garden, let yourself feel that you are leaving the ordinary, everyday world behind… you will continue becoming calmer and more relaxed as you go down each step… you will keep feeling more peaceful and at ease… when you reach the bottom step and walk across that path to the magical garden… without even noticing it, the ordinary world will fade away during this meditation.

So now, please start counting backwards from ten to one and you will go down one step each time you think a number... ten... nine... eight... seven... six... five... four... three... two... and one... you are at the bottom of the stairs, and you are walking across the path toward the garden... the garden is beautiful... the ground soft and springy beneath your feet... birds singing cheerfully... the sunlight streaming through the trees... you find a soft place to lie down... you put your head back and relax completely... you are feeling more and more calm and at ease... feeling yourself absorbing the peace, the stillness and the beauty all around you.

Now I would like for you to concentrate on the word peace... notice as you concentrate on the world peace... that you feel a soothing calmness moving through your entire body... peace... peace... you are beginning to feel as though you are flowing away on a soft, fluffy , white cloud... you are floating out beyond time and space... you are now very comfortable, relaxed and at ease... you are experiencing perfect peace of mind... in the future you can have this calmness and relaxation any time you want it... all you will need to do is sit down or lie down in a comfortable position, close your eyes and imagine yourself in this magical garden... then count backwards in your mind from ten down to one... by the time you reach the number one, you will be relaxed, calm and at ease... you can remain in that state as long as you want to... when you are ready to come back to a wide-awake fully alert state, you will do so immediately just by opening your eyes... you will always feel rested and refreshed, full of energy, strength and vitality after relaxing this way for a few minutes.

Whenever you are ready, you can simply open your eyes, back in a wide awake fully alert state, feeling calm, relaxed and peaceful.

May the following meditation take you to a beautiful place of inner peace:

Please close your eyes and either set a timer or count

from one to five at the end of this meditation, to bring you back completely into a wide awake fully alert state. Please begin to breathe deeply and slowly five times.

Imagine yourself in a peaceful place… your own private, sacred sanctuary… all things are possible in this private peaceful place… as you breathe easily, effortlessly, freely… gentle, soothing , relaxing… you are gifting yourself with this time of peace… going to an inner place of journeying and imagine in your mind's eye that you are lying back in a little boat… you are very, very safe… you are drifting alone a body of water… crystal clear water… feeling very safe, supported and secure… you know you are protected… the boat is very stable… no fears… the mind has let go… you are merely drifting on this body of water… gently and easily.

You lie back and feel the warmth of the sun on your skin… the chimes of bells carry you along… taking you on a magical journey… but where, you do not know… you have no thoughts… no worries… no cares… allowing self to just drift along… feeing very safe… there are beautiful Divine beings around the boat… that is why nothing will happen to you in the boat… you are being safely guided on this journey… you feel lighter and lighter as you drift along in the water… feathers may sprinkle down around you and float on the water… beside the water… little tiny white feathers, symbolic that you too are as light as feather… for you have filled yourself with white light.

You are becoming one with the sound and the water… the most beautiful beings are taking you on this magical journey away from the land of cares and concerns… you are being gently rocked as if you would be in the arms of unconditional love… held safely and securely… you feel the love pour down over you as if the Creator's golden white light is bathing you and embracing you and showering down upon you… the mind has let go of its hold on the earthly plane… for you feel as light as a feather... as the feathers drifting next to you... you feel warm and safe in the golden white light... as you continue to drift on the waters of life... being carried by a gentle current... being rocked and loved, knowing that these energies that gather around you have great love for you and their only concern is for you to relax and feel peaceful... and effect healing and release on all levels... they are here to assist you to do that.

As you continue to float along the water... and finally the little boat brings you safely back home again... beautiful beings assist you to step out of the boat... returning safely home... you are now empowered with the greatest gift of peace... a trust of your inner knowingness... you walk up onto the shore, onto a little path... leading you safely home... aware of a blue light of peace going through every pore, part and particle of your being... gently coming back to where you have been and coming back fully to the present moment aware of this beautiful gift you have given yourself.

Now slowly open your eyes and you are back in a wide, awake, fully alert state, feeling peaceful, and feeling balanced in mind, body and spirit.

As you move through this healing process, you realize that you have within you, in the deepest places, peace. A serenity that abides throughout every situation. This peace abides throughout discouragement, upsets, stress, fear or anxiety. Calmness and peace come from this inner sanctuary.

Through accessing the inner mind and applying the principles within this book, you realize that you have within yourself all that you so desire. You, yourself bring forth your own comfort, safety, confidence, power, wisdom, love, healing, happiness, creativity, successfulness and peace. They all lie deeply within your true self; you need merely to draw upon them at will. Simply reach within and trust what you find.

You can live your life in this way; joyfully, happily, successfully. You are able to go into that deep self anytime you wish, to find the keys to your own truth and to existence itself. Seeing from the vaster perspective of your true self, will you bring you the peace you so desire and deserve. These are the keys to living a life free of anxiety and stress and finding the true self within. These are your own resources, so no one can ever take them from you. These spiritual resources were with you from the beginning and they will be with you always.

My intent and deepest desire is that these words have taken you on a journey to discovering your true inner being. Step by step processes and advice to release those things that no longer serve you and keep you from being relaxed, serene, calm, and at ease. Discovering who you are is a journey everyone deserves to take as the path leads you to healing, new awareness and a life filled with peace.

CONCLUSION

"I wish I could show you when you are lonely or in
darkness the astonishing light of your own being."
~ Hafiz

Readers, I am so honored to have been with you on this
journey in discovering your true self; your true inner being.
As you have learned how to release those layers which
have kept you from being at peace, your life transforms in
powerful and positive ways. You're no longer allowing
what has been to keep you down or stuck in patterns of
anxiety, stress and negativity. It all begins with the discovery of the true self as our initial stage of healing. If we are
not aware of our true self, we are pulled down, trapped and
imprisoned by our negative thoughts, feelings, actions and
experiences.

We identify with that unhealed part of self and believe
that is who we truly are. In that old paradigm we, unfortunately, believe we are the anxiety itself, we are the stress,
we are the depression, we are the anger, we are less than
and so on. Thus, as we start our healing journey to free
ourselves from anxiety, stress, fear, anger, or any negative
beliefs about ourselves, it is essential we recognize that we

do have a true self.

Through daily communication with the unconscious mind, we forge that deep connection to that sense of self. As we delve into the unconscious, we release all that is preventing us from being at peace, and all that is blocking us from reaching our goals and dreams. We cross the bridge between conscious mind into the level of spirit consciousness. As we connect to this part of self on the level of spirit consciousness, we become the observer. In this way, we can clearly see what needs to be healed. We discover who we truly are separate from the anxious, depressed, stressed, not enough, angry thoughts and feelings. Thus providing us with the ability to detach from these unwanted issues and ways of being while illuminating what is blocking our true nature which is always peaceful, wise, loving, and knows our true path and purpose. With this healing, we can begin to undo and release all the painful experiences, the layers of anger, the woundedness of the inner child, the lack of self-love and all which prevents us from being at peace.

Through my experience, I believe that the universal lesson for all readers is to find the spiritual self, the higher self, the true self whatever name you prefer to call it. In this discovery, you realize that you can only find true peace, truth, joy and happiness through reconnecting with your true self and listening to its guidance. Learning this truth, allows you to live your life in joy. Your true self is a perfect instrument through which your soul can express itself fully. As your higher self, you can carry out your soul's purpose, recognizing and bringing forth your true purpose, mission, and passion.

Rather than following the desires of the personality self, you can align with your true self, recognizing the truth which lies within each of us. You can express your uniqueness as your personality self but coming from the wisdom of the higher self, bringing forth a new way of being and responding as you leave the old unwanted patterns of anxiety and stress behind.

As you absorb, filter, integrate, incorporate and utilize the healing tools, words and techniques in this book, you will become aware of a cycle of progress which grows stronger and stronger as each day passes. The mind learns through repetition, so as the tools, techniques, visualizations and meditations are applied on a regular basis, you will learn a new way of being. As you courageously take one breath at a time, one step at a time, old unhealthy, unwanted patterns will gradually let go. As the mind experiences more times of stillness, the true self emerges. Please be very patient and loving with yourself in this healing process. Give yourself a lot of credit for even the most subtle changes. These changes will slowly begin to grow and flourish in your life, becoming a permanent part of you, a permanent part of your personality and reality.

Gradually the old anxious, stressful response patterns lose their grip on your behavior, your thoughts, your feelings and who you thought you were. Through the healing practices provided here, you make a commitment to yourself. You are making a commitment to always be there for yourself, never again letting yourself down or turning your back on yourself. Through addressing the layers of pain, you no longer reject parts of yourself. This gift comes forth from the wounds you are healing. Healing those wounds allows you to see the gift within the pain. That is, that woundedness you've endured brings forth compassion, wisdom, strength, capacities, mastery and empathy. The true self permits you to see those gifts, resources and strengths which lived beneath the pain. They were within you all along. Now you are bringing them forth into every aspect of your life.

Communication with the unconscious mind each day brings forth healing of all four bodies: the physical body, mental body, emotional body and spiritual body. As we clear out blocks held unconsciously, we heal on all these levels. When these four bodies are aligned, the light of the higher self can flow freely through us. The soul heals as well as releases the pain and learns lessons gleaned from painful experiences, becoming clearer, more sure-footed as it moves along in its path and purpose. It also connects us strongly to the Divine. We then see we are never alone, and we can trust in that Divine support always. When our true self offers guidance, we can turn to the Divine and ask for the willingness and courage to take action.

May each chapter take you further and deeper into your true self as you let go of that which no longer serves you. As you dive deeply to the core of yourself, you create a sacred healing space within, a place of peace and safety. You create a sanctuary inside that is quiet, loving, deep, healing and wonderful, allowing you to return to this place always as you allow yourself to experience anything that might be going on inside. You also experience from the perspective of the true self as you witness layers of pain begin to surface which had been beneath the feelings/thoughts of anxiety and stress.

The supreme transformation of darkness into light, using the various practices to help you get in touch with those feelings, allows you to experience it, pay attention to it, release and transform it. Through this transformation, you begin to then get in touch with your inner child who has been there waiting all along. Waiting patiently to be heard, to be seen to be healed. The child brings forth gifts of creativity, spontaneity, playfulness and lightness of being. As this unfolds you begin to feel love, beautiful divine and human love, feeling a sense of safety and protection as thought a blanket of peace were wrapped around you.

As you start to feel your connection to the Divine, you turn to the Divine for support along your journey, deepening your faith in yourself and in in the Divine. Through this healing process, you will know that you are able to move from darkness, anxiety, stress and negativity into light. Everything in you is being transformed. Again, understanding that healing takes place on all three levels of the mind: conscious mind, unconscious mind and all the level of spirit consciousness. All types of challenges are being reframed, released and transformed as they are seen from the perspective of the true self by being able to ultimately transform difficulties into love, wisdom and peace within the light of the true self.

I thank you for sharing this journey of faith, hope and healing with me, and am deeply grateful to you for reading these words and allowing me to share this information. As you heal and release stress and anxiety you let go of negativity and unforgotten pain, please keep these words of encouragement close to your heart, reconnecting you to the part of you that is wise, clear, motivated and Divinely directed. Feeling at peace and taking daily guided action in the direction of your goals and dreams is your birthright. Embracing your true self, your inner authority empowers you take charge of your life. Becoming grateful for all experiences, no matter how unpleasant, allows those experiences to serve as your teachers, now holding the intention of healing and being healed. May these words and teachings carry you along as you bring forth the light of your true self to any pain, anxiety, darkness or wounds. May you see 'when you are lonely or in darkness the astonishing light of your own being.'

ABOUT THE AUTHOR

Mary Sidhwani is a Certified Clinical Hypnotherapist and holds a certification in cancer support. She has had the privilege of helping women overcome a variety of issues including: anxiety, trauma, phobias, depression and panic disorder.

Her educational background includes a Bachelor's Degree in Behavioral Science, a Masters in Clinical Hypnotherapy, and a Doctorate in Psychology.

Mary is also a Registered Nurse and has had more than 15 years experience working with children experiencing abuse and emotional problems, as well as working with the developmentally disabled and developing in-service trainings.

In addition, she is a professional speaker and has presented at institutions such as NASA, Bon Secours Health Systems, W. R. Grace , professional women's groups and general audiences on topics ranging from hypnotherapy , stress management, inner child work, cancer support among other topics. She is also the author of the guided hypnosis audio series:

"Recognize the Truth Within: An Inner Healing Journey for Women." In addition, Mary is a contributing author to the book: "The Heart to Heart Series: The Path to Wellness."

Mary has been in private practice in Ellicott City, Maryland since 2000. She is a member of several professional organizations including: American Society of Clinical Hypnosis, Women in Psychology, American Nurses Association, and the American Board of Hypnotherapy.

www.WomensTherapeutic.com

REFERENCES

1. "Finding your True Self: Using Hypnosis and Other Tools to Uncover the Real You." By Katherine Zimmerman, CHT Trancetime Publishing 2001,2004

2. Relay.nationalgeographic.com "People can hallucinate color at will." Article by Christine Dell 'Amor 12/7/2011

3. "Seven Habits of Effective People." By Stephen R. Covey 11/19/13 Simon and Schuster

4. "Mirror Work: 21 Days to Heal Your Life." By Louise Hay 3/22/16 Hay House

5. "Love, Medicine and Miracles: Lessons Learned About Self-Healing From a Surgeon's Experience with Exceptional Patients." By Bernie S. Siegel, M.D. 8/30/2011 Wm. Morris publishing

6. "Healing the Child Within" by Charles L. Whitefield M.D. 1/1/10 Health Communications Inc.

7. "Your Inner Child of the Past" by W. Hugh Missildine 6/1/63 Simon and Schuster

8. "Betrayal of Innocence" By Susan Forward and Craig Buck 7/1/78 Houghton Mifflin Harcourt

9. "Learning to Love Yourself Workbook." By Gay Hendricks PhD 11/10/90 Atria Books

10. "The Soul of Psychosynthesis: The Seven Core Concepts." By Piero Ferrucci 5/29/16 Kontaur Publishing

11. "Self Hypnosis and other Mind-Expanding Techniques." By Charles Tebbets 6/1/77 Westwood Publishing

12. "Hypnosis: The Mind /Body Connection." By Peter C. Mutke , M.D. Writers House 1987

Made in the USA
Las Vegas, NV
07 September 2021